McGraw-Hill's

500 Series 7
Exam Questions
to Know by Test Day

Also in McGraw-Hill's 500 Questions Series

McGraw-Hill's

500 Series 7 Exam Questions to Know by Test Day

Esmé Faerber

New York Chicago San Francisco Lisbon London Madrid Mexico City
Milan New Delhi San Juan Seoul Singapore Sydney Toronto

The **McGraw·Hill** Companies

Esmé Faerber's financial career began at Citicorp and spans several decades. She is currently a professor at Rosemont College, where she teaches investments and finance.

1 2 3 4 5 6 7 8 9 10 11 12 13 14 15   QFR/QFR   1 9 8 7 6 5 4 3 2

ISBN   978-0-07-178978-3
MHID   0-07-178978-2

e-ISBN   978-0-07-178979-0
e-MHID   0-07-178979-0

Library of Congress Control Number 2012946833

The General Securities Representative Exam (Series 7 exam) is a registered trademark of the Financial Industry Regulatory Authority, which was not involved in the production of, and does not endorse, this product.

This publication is designed to provide accurate and authoritative information in regard to the subject matter covered. It is sold with the understanding that neither the author nor the publisher is engaged in rendering legal, accounting, or other professional services. If legal advice or other expert assistance is required, the services of a competent professional person should be sought.
   —*From a Declaration of Principles Jointly Adopted by a Committee of the American Bar Association and a Committee of Publishers and Associations*

McGraw-Hill products are available at special quantity discounts to use as premiums and sales promotions or for use in corporate training programs. To contact a representative, please e-mail us at bulksales@mcgraw-hill.com.

This book is printed on acid-free paper.

CONTENTS

PREFACE

Congratulations! You've taken a big step toward Series 7 success by purchasing *McGraw-Hill's 500 Series 7 Exam Questions to Know by Test Day*. This book gives you 500 Series 7–style multiple-choice questions that cover the essential material. Each question is clearly explained in the Answer Key. Answering these questions will give you valuable independent practice to supplement your other studies.

No matter what your preparation style (working consistently for months before the exam or doing last-minute preparations), you will benefit from reviewing these 500 questions, which closely parallel the content, format, and degree of difficulty of the questions on the actual Series 7 exam. These questions and the explanations in the Answer Key are the ideal last-minute study tool for those final weeks before the test.

If you practice with all the questions and answers in this book, we are certain you will build the skills and confidence needed to excel on the Series 7 exam. Good luck!

—Editors of McGraw-Hill Education

PREPARING FOR THE EXAM

This book provides you with 500 multiple-choice questions and answers to prepare you to successfully take the Series 7 exam to become a stockbroker. The questions cover the essential course material in the exam, and the answers provide you with detailed definitions, concepts, and formulas, as well as the common mistakes to avoid. If you are not familiar with the theory and concepts, you should go back to your textbooks to understand the underlying theory. Practice on these questions gives you an important supplement to your regular textbook study.

The Series 7 exam is a six-hour, closed-book test consisting of 260 multiple-choice questions. The three-hour morning session covers the first 130 questions, and the remaining 130 questions are covered in the three-hour afternoon session. There are 10 questions asked by the test committee, which have no effect on the candidate's score. In other words, only 250 of the 260 questions asked are scored. A passing score is 70 percent (175 correct answers).

The following table shows a listing of questions from the different functional areas for the Series 7 exam as outlined by the Financial Industry Regulatory Authority (FINRA):

Series 7 Examination Questions

Functional Area	Number of Questions	Exam Percentage
Seeking business for broker-dealer	9	4%
Evaluating customer financial needs/objectives	4	2%
Providing customers with investment information and making suitable recommendations	123	49%
Customer accounts and records	27	11%
Providing an understanding of the securities markets	53	21%
Verifying and processing customer orders and transactions	13	5%
Portfolio analysis, economic and financial analysis	21	8%
Total	250	100%

Source: Financial Industry Regulatory Authority

Many of the questions asked in the exam overlap these functional areas, and so the chapters in this book are organized into the different financial securities (stocks, bonds, options, mutual funds), account management and trading, underwriting securities, exchange markets, portfolio and securities analysis, and rules and regulations.

Practice your test-taking skills by budgeting your time for each question. In the Series 7 exam you have three hours for 130 questions, or approximately one minute and 20 seconds to answer each question. Consequently, when you practice answering the multiple-choice questions in this book, get into the habit of spending no more than one minute and 20 seconds per question. The following time allocations for the number of questions answered may be useful for you to be aware of when you take the examination:

Number of Questions You Should Answer	Time Limit
10 questions	13 minutes
20 questions	27 minutes
30 questions	41 minutes
40 questions	55 minutes
44 questions	60 minutes

A few tips about taking tests:

- Do not dwell on a question that you do not know for longer than the time indicated above (one minute and 20 seconds).
- If you don't know the answer to a question, mark the question on your scrap paper (it is a computerized test) and come back to it when and if you have more time. It is important to budget your time to try to answer all the questions asked.
- Read the questions carefully. Be sure to determine what the question is asking and not what you think the question should be asking. As I always mention to my students, "It is the questions that are difficult, not the answers, which are in front of you in multiple choice!"

Good luck with the exam!

Esmé Faerber

CHAPTER 1

Common Stock and Preferred Stock

1. The book value of common stock is the same as

    (A) par value
    (B) liquidation value
    (C) net worth
    (D) net tangible asset value per share

2. At the company's shareholder meeting, five positions are up for election to the board of directors. Jason Smart owns 200 shares, and voting is on a cumulative basis. Which of the following are acceptable ways for Jason to vote?

    I. 200 votes for each of the five candidates
    II. 1,000 votes for one candidate
    III. 600 votes for one candidate and 100 votes for each of the other four candidates
    IV. 1,000 votes for each candidate

    (A) I, II, and IV
    (B) I only
    (C) I, III, and IV
    (D) I, II, and III

3. ABC Corporation issues new shares to its existing shareholders through a rights offering. The stock is offered to its existing shareholders at $20 per share and eight rights. The market price of ABC stock is $26 per share. What is the value of a cum-right?

    (A) $0.67
    (B) $0.75
    (C) $1.33
    (D) $1.50

4. Four directors are to be elected under the statutory method. If a shareholder owns 100 shares, how would he or she cast these votes?
   I. 400 votes for one director
   II. 100 votes for each director
   III. 300 votes for one director and 100 votes for one director

   (A) I, II, and III
   (B) I and III
   (C) II only
   (D) I and II

5. WAZ Corporation's stock trades ex-dividend on Tuesday, April 8. If a shareholder would like to receive the dividend, on which day should the investor purchase the stock?

   (A) Friday, April 4
   (B) Thursday, April 3
   (C) Wednesday, April 2
   (D) Monday, April 7

6. Treasury stock is considered to be

   (A) authorized and issued shares
   (B) issued and outstanding shares
   (C) authorized and unissued shares
   (D) unissued and outstanding shares

7. The ex-dividend date for trading common stock is

   (A) two business days after the record date
   (B) two business days before the record date
   (C) one business day before the record date
   (D) one business day after the record date

8. Which of the following statements about a limit order to sell stock is true?

   (A) If the market price of the stock trades at or above the limit price, the order will be executed.
   (B) If the market price of the stock trades below the limit price, the order will be executed.
   (C) Once the limit order is triggered, the order could be filled below the limit price.
   (D) None of the above

9. Which of the following ratios indicates high leverage for a corporation?
   (A) High working capital
   (B) High current ratio
   (C) High gross margin
   (D) High debt-to-equity ratio

10. XYZ Corporation has 5,000,000 common shares and 1,000,000 shares of 6 percent $100 par value cumulative preferred stock. During the recession of the past two years, XYZ suspended all dividend payments. This year XYZ returned to profitability, and the board of directors declared a $1 per share common stock dividend to be paid at the end of the year. How much would XYZ have to pay in dividends this year?
   (A) $5,000,000
   (B) $11,000,000
   (C) $17,000,000
   (D) $23,000,000

11. A technical analyst is most concerned with which of the following?
   I. EPS
   II. P/E ratio
   III. Resistance and support levels
   IV. Market timing
   (A) I, II, and IV
   (B) IV only
   (C) III and IV
   (D) III only

12. A fundamental analyst is least concerned with
   (A) short interest ratio
   (B) earnings per share
   (C) industry analysis
   (D) cash flow analysis

13. A stock has a beta coefficient of 1.10. What does this mean?
   (A) This stock is less volatile than the market.
   (B) If the market goes up, this stock is expected to decline in price.
   (C) If the market goes up, this stock should increase in price.
   (D) If the market goes down, this stock should decline by less than the percentage decline of the market.

14. Which of the following information cannot be determined from the balance sheet alone?
    (A) Current ratio
    (B) Debt-to-equity ratio
    (C) Return on equity
    (D) Retained earnings

Questions 15 and 16 are based on the following information:

The ticker tape for XYZ Corporation's stock shows the following:

    36.10, 36.20, 36.50, 36.00, 36.10, 36.20

An investor initiates a sell stop order for 100 shares of XYZ at 36.00.

15. At what price was the order triggered?
    (A) 36.10
    (B) 36.20
    (C) 36.50
    (D) 36.00

16. At what price was the order executed?
    (A) 36.10
    (B) 36.20
    (C) 36.50
    (D) 36.00

17. A specialist holds which type of orders in his or her book?
    I. Stop orders
    II. Limit orders
    III. Market orders
    IV. Not-held orders

    (A) I and II
    (B) II and III
    (C) I, II, and III
    (D) II and IV

18. Which type of investment is most suitable for an investor to invest in for an infant child's future college education?
    (A) Junk bonds
    (B) Treasury bonds
    (C) Blue-chip stocks
    (D) Speculative stocks

19. XYZ Corporation issues new shares but decides not to sell them all. Under a shelf registration, XYZ can sell the shares held back within the next _____ without having to reregister them.

(A) two years
(B) one year
(C) 270 days
(D) None of the above

20. A trade involving two institutions that do not use the services of a broker-dealer takes place in the

(A) first market
(B) second market
(C) third market
(D) fourth market

21. Stocks with high P/E ratios that do NOT pay or pay low dividends would be typical of

(A) value stocks
(B) blue-chip stocks
(C) growth stocks
(D) utility company stocks

22. A 5.5 percent preferred stock with a $100 par value is trading at $80 per share and is callable at $101 per share. What is its nominal yield?

(A) 6.88 percent
(B) 5.45 percent
(C) 5.5 percent
(D) None of the above

23. An investor owns 2,000 shares of XYZ Corporation and decides to sell 1,000 shares. Which statement about the sale is true?

(A) The investor can specify which shares are to be sold in order to minimize capital gains.
(B) The investor must use the LIFO method to identify which shares are to be sold.
(C) The investor must use the FIFO method to identify which shares are to be sold.
(D) The investor does not have a choice in determining which of the shares are to be sold.

24. The pink sheets provide
    I. quotes for stocks listed on NASDAQ
    II. quotes for exchange-listed stocks
    III. wholesale quotes for OTC stocks that are thinly traded or too small to be listed on NASDAQ
    IV. the names of the market makers for OTC stocks

    (A) I and IV
    (B) II and IV
    (C) III and IV
    (D) I and III

Questions 25 and 26 are based on the following information:

Balance Sheet information for XYZ Corporation as of December 31, 20XX, and Income Statement information for the year ended December 31, 20XX

Cash	$5,000,000
Depreciation	$500,000
Interest expense	$100,000
Operating profit (EBIT)	$4,000,000
Taxation	40%
Preferred dividends	250,000
Common stock dividends	200,000
Number of shares outstanding	1,000,000
Market price of the common stock	$15

25. What is the price/earnings ratio?
    (A) 7.94
    (B) 7.18
    (C) 0.14
    (D) 6.41

26. What is the cash flow per share?
    (A) $5.00
    (B) $4.50
    (C) $2.84
    (D) $2.09

27. If an investor wants a specified price or better when buying and selling stocks, which types of orders should he or she place?
    (A) Buy stops and sell stops
    (B) Buy limits and sell limits
    (C) Buy stops and sell limits
    (D) Buy limits and sell stops

28. XYZ Corporation has a 6 percent participating preferred stock issue, along with a common stock issue. Which of the following statements is true?
    (A) Participating preferred shareholders receive a minimum dividend payment of 6 percent.
    (B) Participating preferred shareholders receive an average dividend payment of 6 percent.
    (C) Participating preferred shareholders receive only 6 percent in dividends.
    (D) Participating preferred shareholders receive a maximum dividend payment of 6 percent.

29. An investor bought 1,000 shares of XZ Corporation's common stock at $35 per share and paid a total commission of $20 for the trade. If XZ issues a 10 percent stock dividend, which of the following statements is true after the stock dividend?
    (A) The investor has 1,100 shares at a cost basis of $35.02 per share.
    (B) The investor has 1,000 shares at a cost basis of $35.02 per share.
    (C) The investor has 1,100 shares at a cost basis of $31.84 per share.
    (D) The investor has 1,000 shares at a cost basis of $31.84 per share.

30. A company whose stock trades at $40 per share and has earnings per share of $5 decides on a 2-for-1 stock split. After the stock split, which of the following statements is true?
    I. The earnings per share is $5.
    II. The earnings per share is $2.50.
    III. The price/earnings ratio is 8.
    IV. The price/earnings ratio is 4.

    (A) I and III
    (B) II and IV
    (C) I and IV
    (D) II and III

31. Which of the following statements about ADRs is true?

(A) They assist foreign investors in investing in U.S. stocks.
(B) They assist U.S. investors in investing in foreign stocks.
(C) They assist U.S. investors in investing in U.S. stocks.
(D) They assist foreign investors in investing in foreign stocks.

32. Which of the following actions does NOT decrease working capital?

(A) Paying off long-term bonds three years before the maturity date
(B) Declaring a dividend
(C) Paying a dividend
(D) Buying machinery for cash

33. Which of the following statements about an advance-decline line used by technical analysts best portrays its use?

(A) Shows the volatility of the market
(B) Shows the integrity of the market
(C) Shows the volume of stocks traded in the market
(D) Shows the direction of the market

Questions 34 and 35 are based on the following information:

A computer shows the following information for XYZZ, a NASDAQ-listed stock:

L	6.12	O	5.85	C	6.10
B	6	H	6.15	NC	+ .20
A	6.15	L	5.85	V	320

34. What is the quote for XYZZ stock?

(A) 6.10 - 6.12
(B) 5.85 - 6.15
(C) 6 - 6.10
(D) 6 - 6.15

35. If an investor placed a limit order to sell XYZZ at 6.12 when the stock traded at 6.15, why was the order NOT executed?

(A) The stock never traded above 6.
(B) The last trade was 5.85.
(C) The stock traded at 6.15 on the previous day.
(D) The trade at 6.15 was by another market maker.

36. What determines the yield on common stock?
   I. Earnings
   II. Dividends paid
   III. Number of shares outstanding
   IV. Market price of the stock

   (A) I and III
   (B) II and IV
   (C) I, II, and IV
   (D) III and IV

37. If a company sells newly issued $5 million, 6 percent debenture bonds maturing in 2040, which of the following balance sheet accounts will increase?
   I. Current liabilities
   II. Total liabilities
   III. Current assets
   IV. Net worth

   (A) I and III
   (B) I, II, and III
   (C) II, III, and IV
   (D) II and III

38. The support level is

   (A) the lower level of a stock's trading range
   (B) the upper level of a stock's trading range
   (C) the middle level of a stock's trading range
   (D) None of the above

39. A stock has a P/E ratio of 15 when the market price is $60 per share. What is the company's EPS?

   (A) $0.25
   (B) $4.00
   (C) $1.00
   (D) Cannot be determined from the information provided

40. An investor owns 1,000 shares of XYZ Corporation when the corporation announces a 1-for-4 reverse stock split. Before the stock split, XYZ's stock was trading at $1.50 per share. After the stock split, what ownership position will the investor have?

(A) 4,000 shares at $0.37 per share
(B) 1,000 shares at $6.00 per share
(C) 250 shares at $1.50 per share
(D) 250 shares at $6.00 per share

41. Which of the following trades of 770 shares is NOT good delivery for a trade?

(A) One certificate of 700 shares and one certificate of 70 shares
(B) Two certificates of 300 shares, one certificate of 100 shares, and one certificate of 70 shares
(C) Nine certificates of 70 shares, one certificate of 50 shares, and one certificate of 90 shares
(D) Three certificates of 200 shares, one certificate of 100 shares, and one certificate of 70 shares

42. A corporation has 6 percent participating preferred stock. What does the 6 percent mean?

(A) Maximum dividend payment
(B) Minimum dividend payment
(C) Actual dividend payment
(D) None of the above

43. Shareholders of a corporation must approve which of the following?
   I. Giving shareholders a stock dividend
  II. Giving shareholders a cash dividend
 III. Splitting the stock
  IV. Reverse-splitting the stock

(A) I and II only
(B) III and IV only
(C) All of the above
(D) None of the above

44. One of your clients is interested in equity investments that pay dividends. Which of the following investments would you NOT recommend?

(A) XYZ common stock
(B) XYZ preferred stock
(C) XYZ convertible preferred stock
(D) XYZ warrants

CHAPTER 2

Bonds

45. An investor buys fifty 6 percent coupon bonds at $101, maturing in 20 years. The bonds are currently trading at $102. How much semiannual interest will the investor receive?

(A) $3,030
(B) $1,530
(C) $3,000
(D) $1,500

46. An investor purchases a bond with a coupon yield of 4 percent maturing in six years. If the yield-to-maturity on the bond is 4.9 percent, how much did the investor pay for the bond?

(A) Above $1,000
(B) Below $1,000
(C) $1,000
(D) Cannot determine the price from the information presented

47. An investor purchased a 4 percent coupon bond, maturing in 10 years, at 85. The investor holds the bond for five years and sells it at 90. What is the investor's gain or loss?

(A) $50 gain
(B) $500 gain
(C) $100 loss
(D) $25 loss

48. Which of the following is NOT a money market security?

(A) Commercial paper
(B) Treasury bills
(C) Treasury notes
(D) CDs

49. Determine the tax consequences of the following transaction: An investor purchases five convertible bonds at 93 and a week later converts the bonds into common stock. The conversion price is $40, and the investor sells the shares at $38 per share.

    (A) $20 capital gain
    (B) $20 capital loss
    (C) $100 capital gain
    (D) $100 capital loss

50. An investor purchases a 4.5 percent bond at 90 that matures in 10 years. What is the tax liability of this bond?

    (A) $45
    (B) $35
    (C) $55
    (D) $145

51. Which of the following is NOT true with regard to a bond that is selling at a premium?

    (A) The nominal yield is greater than the current yield.
    (B) The market price of the bond is greater than the face value of the bond.
    (C) The yield-to-maturity is greater than the current yield.
    (D) Market rates of interest more than likely increased after this bond is issued.

Questions 52 and 53 are based on the following information:

A company issues 5 percent convertible bonds maturing in eight years. The bonds were sold at 80 per bond.

52. An investor purchased five of these bonds. What is the investor's current yield?

    (A) 5 percent
    (B) 6.25 percent
    (C) 7.25 percent
    (D) None of the above

53. In decreasing order, the yields are

    (A) yield-to-maturity, current, and nominal
    (B) yield-to-maturity, nominal, and current
    (C) nominal, current, and yield-to-maturity
    (D) current, nominal, and yield-to-maturity

54. The balance sheet of XYZ Corporation shows $1,000,000 of callable bonds with a conversion price of $33 and $1 par value common stock of $2,000,000. If net income is $2,300,000, then what is the earnings per share?

(A) $2.00
(B) $1.15
(C) $1.00
(D) $0.87

55. An investor buys a Treasury bond on Tuesday, June 5. How many days of accrued interest must the investor pay if the Treasury bond last paid interest on March 15?

(A) 80 days
(B) 81 days
(C) 82 days
(D) 83 days

56. Which statements are true about Treasury STRIP securities?

   I. Investors pay taxes on interest earned at maturity.
  II. Investors pay taxes on annual interest earned.
 III. Investors receive semiannual interest payments.
 IV. Investors are paid principal and interest at maturity.

(A) I and II
(B) I and III
(C) II and IV
(D) I and IV

57. If interest rates are expected to increase over the next decade, which types of investments would you advise an investor to make?

(A) 20-year Treasury bonds
(B) 20-year zero-coupon bonds
(C) 20-year corporate bonds
(D) 6-month Treasury bills

58. A quote of 102.04 for a 20-year Treasury bond in dollar amounts is

(A) $102.04
(B) $1,020.25
(C) $1,021.25
(D) $1,020.40

59. Which of the following securities are NOT quoted in 32nds?

(A) GNMAs
(B) Treasury notes
(C) Treasury bills
(D) FNMAs

60. An investor seeking the highest return from a typical "plain vanilla" CMO would invest in the

(A) principal-only tranche
(B) interest-only tranche
(C) first tranche
(D) last tranche

61. Which of the following best describes the purpose of the Federal National Mortgage Association?

(A) Lends mortgage money directly to qualified veterans
(B) Sets mortgage rates and terms for qualified buyers of property
(C) Promotes liquidity in the secondary mortgage market
(D) All of the above

62. Which types of risk are avoided when investing in zero-coupon bonds?
  I. Inflation risk
  II. Interest rate risk
  III. Credit risk
  IV. Reinvestment rate risk

(A) I and II
(B) II and III
(C) III and IV
(D) II and IV

63. Investors in GNMA pass-through securities receive

(A) monthly payments of interest
(B) monthly payments of interest and principal
(C) monthly interest and principal at maturity
(D) interest on a quarterly basis

64. Treasury Inflation Protection Securities (TIPS) face the greatest erosion to principal from which of the following?
  I. Rising interest rates in the economy
  II. Declining interest rates in the economy
  III. Increasing inflation
  IV. Decreasing inflation

  (A) I and III
  (B) II and IV
  (C) I and IV
  (D) II and III

65. What is the price of a Treasury bill sold with a discount yield of 1 percent with a maturity of 180 days?

  (A) $995
  (B) $990
  (C) $950
  (D) $900

66. An investor wishing to protect an investment against rising inflation should invest in

  (A) Treasury bills
  (B) Treasury notes
  (C) Treasury bonds
  (D) common stock

67. All of the following bond securities trade flat EXCEPT

  (A) income bonds
  (B) Treasury bills
  (C) bonds in default
  (D) Treasury inflation protection securities

68. XYZ Corporation has a 6 percent convertible debt issue, which is convertible at 50. The bonds are trading at 110.50 and are callable at 106. The stock is currently trading at 55. Which statements about parity of the bond to the common stock are correct if an investor does NOT convert the bonds?
    I. Parity of the bond to the common stock is 1100.
    II. Parity of the bond to the common stock is 1166.
    III. The market price is 0.50 points above parity.
    IV. The market price is 5.50 points below parity.

    (A) I and IV
    (B) I and III
    (C) II and III
    (D) II and IV

69. Investors investing in CMOs would price them on their

    (A) stated maturities
    (B) stated yields
    (C) prepayment risks
    (D) expected average lives

70. In bankruptcy, holders of subordinated debenture bonds would be paid

    (A) after preferred stockholders
    (B) before secured bondholders
    (C) before existing unsecured bondholders
    (D) after secured and unsecured bondholders but before preferred stockholders

71. A convertible bond with a 5 percent coupon is trading at 106. If the conversion price is 25 and the underlying stock is trading at 27, which of the following statements is true?

    (A) The bond is trading at parity.
    (B) The stock is trading below parity.
    (C) The stock is trading above parity.
    (D) The bond should not be converted.

72. A retiree who is investing for income would least likely invest in

    (A) income bonds
    (B) mortgage bonds
    (C) collateral trust bonds
    (D) equipment trust bonds

73. What is the highest Standard & Poor's speculative bond rating?

   (A) A
   (B) BBB
   (C) BB
   (D) B

74. Which of the following statements about the refunding of a bond issue is NOT true?

   (A) It changes the maturities of the debt structure.
   (B) The corporation does not receive any cash.
   (C) Interest costs are lowered.
   (D) It changes the debt-to-equity ratio.

75. Which of the following securities has the greatest market risk?

   (A) EE savings bonds
   (B) Treasury bills
   (C) CDs
   (D) Treasury notes

76. Commercial paper is normally issued with maturities not exceeding

   (A) one year
   (B) 270 days
   (C) 180 days
   (D) 90 days

77. Which of the following is a bid-ask quote for a Treasury bill?

   (A) 1.05 - 1.03
   (B) 1.03 - 1.05
   (C) 99.6 - 99.8
   (D) 99.8 - 99.9

78. Which of the following statements on Treasury bills is NOT true?

   (A) Interest from Treasury bills is exempt from state taxes.
   (B) Interest from Treasury bills is exempt from federal taxes.
   (C) Treasury bills are always sold at a discount.
   (D) Treasury bills are highly liquid securities.

79. A company wants to sell 1,000 U.S. agency bonds from its investment portfolio. The company receives a quote of 95.04 bid and 95.08 ask. How much will the company receive if it sells these bonds to the securities dealer?

(A) $951,250
(B) $952,500
(C) $950,400
(D) $950,800

80. Which of the following statements about repurchase agreements is NOT true?

(A) A repo is the sale of securities with an agreement to buy them back at the same price at an agreed-upon date in the future.
(B) A repo is the sale of securities with an agreement to buy them back at a higher price at an agreed-upon date in the future.
(C) The difference in the price negotiated between the parties is the amount of interest.
(D) A repo is a money market security with maturities ranging from a few days up to one year.

81. Which type of securities does NOT earn interest?
   I. Treasury bills
   II. Treasury notes
   III. Treasury STRIPs
   IV. Treasury stock

(A) I, II, and III
(B) III and IV
(C) III only
(D) IV only

82. Which of the following statements is NOT true regarding a bond selling at a premium?

(A) The yield-to-maturity is less than the nominal yield.
(B) The current yield is less than the nominal yield.
(C) The bond is trading at a premium price because market rates of interest increased after the bond was issued.
(D) The price of the bond is greater than its face value.

83. If interest rates are expected to decline over the next decade, which types of investments would you suggest for an investor?

    I.   10-year bonds with a put option exercisable in 5 years

    II. Adjustable rate bonds

    III. 10-year noncallable bonds

    IV. 20-year bonds callable in 10 years

    (A) I, II, and IV

    (B) II, III, and IV

    (C) I and III

    (D) I and IV

84. Which type of bond issue is exempt from state taxes for individual investors?

    (A) GNMAs

    (B) Corporate bonds

    (C) Treasury bonds

    (D) Commercial paper

85. A sinking fund provision is typically found in which of the following types of bonds?

    (A) Term bonds

    (B) Mortgage bonds

    (C) Serial bonds

    (D) Bonds requiring a balloon payment

86. Which of the following statements about the concept of duration is NOT true?

    (A) A bond with a duration of 2.45 means that a bondholder will collect the average of the principal and interest payments for this bond in 2.45 years.

    (B) For bonds that pay regular interest payments, duration is always less than the maturity.

    (C) The higher the coupon of the bond, the higher is the duration.

    (D) For zero-coupon bonds, duration is equal to the bond's maturity.

87. The Trust Indenture Act of 1939 covers which of the following bonds?

    (A) Treasury bonds

    (B) Revenue bonds

    (C) Debenture bonds

    (D) Agency bonds

88. What is the normal Standard & Poor's rating of a CMO?

(A) AAA
(B) AA
(C) A
(D) BBB

89. Which statement is true about regular way settlements on government securities?

(A) Settlement takes place three business days after the trade date.
(B) Settlement takes place two business days after the trade date.
(C) Settlement takes place one business day after the trade date.
(D) Settlement takes place on the trade date.

90. The Federal Reserve Bank does NOT set initial margin requirements for which of the following securities?

(A) Common stocks listed on the NASDAQ national market system
(B) Preferred stock
(C) Zero-coupon corporate bonds
(D) Government bonds

91. Which of the following is NOT a money market security?

(A) ADRs
(B) Treasury bills
(C) Repos
(D) CDs

92. Series EE Bonds are sold at what percentage of their face value?

(A) 10 percent
(B) 25 percent
(C) 50 percent
(D) 100 percent

93. Which of the following securities do NOT trade in the secondary market?

  I. ADRs
 II. Repurchase agreements
III. Fed funds
IV. Bankers' acceptances

(A) I and II
(B) II and III
(C) III and IV
(D) I and IV

94. An investor purchases a 6 percent callable bond at 75 with 10 years to maturity. How much should this investor report for tax purposes?

(A) $6
(B) $60
(C) $75
(D) $85

95. Which of the following tranches in a CMO is considered to be the safest?

(A) TAC
(B) PAC
(C) Z
(D) Companion

CHAPTER 3

Municipal Bonds

96. Rank the following municipal bonds in order from the most risky to the least risky.

I. Public housing authority bonds

II. Industrial development revenue bonds

III. Moral obligation bonds

IV. Revenue bonds

(A) II, I, IV, III

(B) I, III, IV, II

(C) III, IV, II, I

(D) II, IV, III, I

97. Revenue bonds typically provide construction money for various projects EXCEPT

(A) public schools

(B) airports

(C) toll highways

(D) pollution control facilities

98. A municipality has 6 percent bonds outstanding, callable in five years. The municipality issues new 4 percent bonds and escrows the funds to be used to call in the bonds in five years. The 6 percent bonds are said to be

I. defaulted

II. defeased

III. refunded

IV. prerefunded

(A) I and IV

(B) I and III

(C) II and III

(D) II and IV

99. Which is the best after-tax yield for an investor in the 28 percent marginal tax bracket?

(A) 3 percent Treasury note
(B) 3.5 percent AAA-rated corporate bond
(C) 2.75 percent Pennsylvania Health System bond
(D) 3.75 percent GNMA security

100. A municipality issued a revenue bond issue under a net revenue pledge. When revenues are received, which expenses will be paid first?

(A) Principal and interest
(B) Reserve maintenance fund
(C) Operation and maintenance
(D) Renewal and replacement fund

101. An investor purchased five municipal bonds at 105 per bond; the bonds have a maturity of 20 years. If the investor sells the bonds at 99 after holding them for 10 years, what is the loss for tax purposes?

(A) $25 per bond
(B) $35 per bond
(C) $50 per bond
(D) $60 per bond

102. An investor purchases a 5 percent municipal bond on December 9 in a regular way trade. The bond pays interest on January 1 and July 1. For how many days of accrued interest would the buyer pay the seller?

(A) 160 days
(B) 161 days
(C) 162 days
(D) 164 days

103. An investor purchases a municipal bond with a remaining maturity of 10 years at 105. The investor holds the bond for six years and sells the bond for 103. What is the capital gain or loss?

(A) $20 loss
(B) $20 gain
(C) $10 loss
(D) $10 gain

104. What are the tax consequences for an investor who purchased a new municipal bond at 95 with a maturity of 10 years and sold the bond at 97.5 after 5 years?

(A) $25 loss

(B) $25 gain

(C) $50 loss

(D) No loss or gain

105. The credit rating of an industrial development revenue bond is based on an analysis of the creditworthiness of the

(A) issuer

(B) lessee

(C) underwriter

(D) bond attorney

106. A double-barreled municipal bond is

(A) a municipal bond backed by the federal government

(B) a corporate bond backed by the federal government

(C) a bond exempt from federal and state taxes

(D) a bond backed by the full faith and credit of the issuing municipality if there are insufficient revenues from the project

107. The source of debt service payments on general obligation bonds issued by a school district is most likely to come from

(A) excise taxes

(B) income taxes

(C) real estate taxes

(D) sales taxes

108. Under MSRB rules, municipal securities dealers

   I. cannot give customers gifts valued at more than $100 per year

  II. can pay legitimate business expenses

 III. enforce all rules

 IV. All of the above

(A) I and II

(B) I and III

(C) II and III

(D) IV only

109. When a municipality issues new bonds through a competitive offering, what should the official notice of sale published by the municipality include?

    I. The bidding details of the offering
    II. The allotment for each syndicate member
    III. The amount of the good faith deposit
    IV. The re-offering yield

    (A) I and II
    (B) I and III
    (C) II and IV
    (D) III and IV

110. Which of the following best describes what a municipal bond broker's broker does?

    I. Trades securities from inventory
    II. Makes a market in securities
    III. Specializes in trading securities with banks and municipal brokers
    IV. Assists municipal dealers in selling their unsold portions of a municipal bond issue

    (A) I, II, III, and IV
    (B) II, III, and IV
    (C) III and IV
    (D) I and II

111. Notes issued by municipalities are most likely issued for which purposes?

    (A) Long-term financing needs
    (B) Short-term needs
    (C) Construction of pollution control facilities
    (D) Construction of sports facilities

112. Which of the following investments is least likely to be purchased by a qualified pension fund?

    (A) Treasury bonds
    (B) Stocks
    (C) Government National Mortgage Association bonds
    (D) Municipal bonds

113. Municipal double-barreled bonds would most likely be rated and traded like

(A) U.S. agency bonds
(B) Treasury bonds
(C) general obligation bonds
(D) revenue bonds

114. Under a net revenue pledge, what is the debt service coverage ratio for a municipality that receives $6,000,000 in revenues and pays $3,000,000 in operating expenses, $1,000,000 in principal, and $500,000 in interest?

(A) 4 to 1
(B) 2 to 1
(C) 1.5 to 1
(D) 1 to 1

115. From highest priority to lowest priority, what is the normal order for filling orders received by a syndicate on a new municipal bond issue?

I. Member
II. Syndicate
III. Presale
IV. Designated

(A) III, II, IV, I
(B) III, IV, II, I
(C) II, IV, III, I
(D) I, IV, III, II

116. Which of the following is NOT part of a municipal bond trader's activities?

(A) Position a firm's inventory
(B) Enter offers for securities
(C) Request bids for different securities
(D) Rate the creditworthiness of municipal bonds

117. Which of the following agencies enforce MSRB rules?

I. MSRB
II. SEC
III. NASD
IV. Controller of the Currency

(A) I and II
(B) I and III
(C) II, III, and IV
(D) I, II, and III

118. Which of the following forms is least likely to be associated with the underwriting of a municipal bond issue?

(A) Best efforts
(B) Competitive bid
(C) Negotiated
(D) Firm commitment

119. Which of the following are the ratings from best to worst for municipal notes?

 I. MIG 1, MIG 2, MIG 3, MIG 4
 II. S&P's AAA, AA, A, BBB, and so on
III. Fitch's F-1, F-2, F-3
IV. S&P's SP-1, SP-2, SP-3

(A) I and II
(B) I, II, and III
(C) I, III, and IV
(D) II, III, and IV

120. A syndicate with 10 equally participating members underwrites $10,000,000 of municipal bonds. Firm X, one of the syndicate members, sells all of its allocated bonds. If the syndicate agreement was set up on a Western account basis and $1,000,000 bonds of syndicate members remain unsold, what is Firm X's responsibility with regard to the unsold bonds?

(A) $100,000 bonds
(B) $200,000 bonds
(C) $1,000,000 bonds
(D) No responsibility

121. How are the benefits from a group net order shared by municipal syndicate members?

(A) Based on the number of orders they have received
(B) Based on the number of presale orders they have received
(C) Based on a member's percentage participation in the account
(D) Equally

122. Which of the following would NOT provide sources of information about new offerings of municipal bonds?

(A) Newspapers
(B) *Bond Buyer*
(C) Munifacts
(D) Blue List

Questions 123–125 are based on the following information:

A 6 percent municipal bond that matures in 10 years has an ask price of 90.

123. What is the nominal yield?

    (A) 7.37 percent
    (B) 6.67 percent
    (C) 6 percent
    (D) 5.88 percent

124. What is the current yield?

    (A) 7.37 percent
    (B) 6.67 percent
    (C) 6 percent
    (D) 5.88 percent

125. What is the yield-to-maturity on this bond?

    (A) 7.37 percent
    (B) 6.67 percent
    (C) 6 percent
    (D) 5.88 percent

126. Which of the following investments would grant investors state tax-free income status in every state of the United States?

    I. Puerto Rico bonds
    II. General obligation bonds
    III. GNMA bonds
    IV. Treasury bonds

    (A) I, II, and III
    (B) II and III
    (C) I and IV
    (D) III and IV

127. If you sell out of your firm's inventory municipal bonds to a client, which of the following is NOT true?
   I. The amount of the commission must be disclosed when the confirmation is sent to the client.
  II. You must disclose the bond ratings in the confirmation letter.
 III. You are required to mark up the bonds before assessing the amount of the commission.
 IV. You should take the total amount of the bonds sold in calculating the amount of the markup.
  (A) I, II, and III
  (B) II, III, and IV
  (C) I, III, and IV
  (D) I, II, and IV

128. What is the first action of a municipal bond syndicate in preparing a bid?
  (A) Prepare the offering scale
  (B) Determine the concession
  (C) Determine the gross spread
  (D) Determine the takedown

129. A municipal bond representative during his or her 90-day apprenticeship may NOT offer
  (A) quotations to other dealers
  (B) bonds to other dealers
  (C) bonds to the public
  (D) new municipal bond issues to security dealers

130. A property with a market value of $600,000 has an assessed value of $500,000. If the tax rate mills are 30, what is the ad valorem tax?
  (A) $15,000
  (B) $18,000
  (C) $1,500
  (D) $1,800

131. Which of the following actions would NOT assist an investor in diversifying a municipal bond portfolio?
  (A) Buying municipal bonds of different issuers
  (B) Buying municipal bonds with different maturities
  (C) Buying larger quantities of bonds held in the portfolio
  (D) Buying municipal bonds of different quality

132. Interest rates are expected to increase due to increasing inflation. Which type of investment would you suggest to an investor?

(A) Long-term municipal bonds
(B) Intermediate-term municipal bonds
(C) Short-term municipal bonds
(D) Money market municipal securities

133. Which of the following is NOT true regarding special assessment bonds?

(A) These bonds are backed by taxes on the projects that benefit from the improvements.
(B) They are considered to be revenue bonds.
(C) They are considered to be a type of general obligation bond.
(D) These bonds are issued to fund projects such as the construction of sewers and streets.

134. Which of the following prepares the legal opinion for a municipal bond issue?

(A) Municipality issuing the bonds
(B) Syndicate manager of the issue
(C) Bond attorney
(D) None of the above

135. When can a municipal bond securities dealer issue a guarantee against losses to a customer in the market value of the bonds?

(A) Only if the bonds are insured
(B) Only if the bonds are AAA rated
(C) Only in the case of a written agreement to that effect
(D) Under no circumstances

136. Which of the following is true concerning special tax bonds?
  I. They are issued by the federal government.
 II. They are backed by sales taxes on tobacco and alcohol.
III. They are backed by property taxes.
 IV. They are backed by excise taxes.

(A) I and III
(B) II and IV
(C) I and II
(D) III and IV

137. Which of the following items are included in a confirmation of a municipal bond transaction?

    I. Any accrued interest

    II. Whether the bonds have been called or prerefunded

    III. Anything unusual about the bonds

    IV. The broker-dealer's name and address.

    (A) I, II, III, and IV

    (B) I, II, and IV

    (C) II, III, and IV

    (D) I and II

138. Which statement about municipal bonds is NOT true?

    (A) Municipalities provide an official statement for new issues of municipal bonds.

    (B) Municipalities must provide a prospectus for new issues of municipal bonds.

    (C) Municipal bonds are exempt from the registration requirements under the Securities Act of 1933.

    (D) The official statement also includes the underwriting spread, the offering terms, the legal opinion, and information about the municipality and how the funds will be repaid.

139. The rate covenant on a revenue bond for a toll facility negotiated by the issuer and the bondholders would cover what percentage of the facility's debt service payments and maintenance charges?

    (A) 50 percent

    (B) 75 percent

    (C) 80 percent

    (D) 120 percent

140. Which of the following municipal bond issues, all trading at a 5.25 basis, is most likely to be refunded?

    (A) 7.5 percent coupon callable at 100 in 2014

    (B) 6.75 percent coupon callable at 103 in 2013

    (C) 6.5 percent coupon callable at 102 in 2013

    (D) 6 percent coupon callable at 101 in 2012

141. Which of the following best defines the placement ratio for municipal securities?

(A) The total dollar amount of the new issue municipal securities expected to be issued over the next 30 days

(B) The total dollar amount of new municipal securities placed by underwriting syndicates in the past 30 days

(C) The amount of new issue municipal securities sold to underwriting syndicates in the prior two weeks

(D) The amount of new issue municipal securities sold to underwriting syndicates in the past week

142. Which of the following circumstances would be considered positive in analyzing whether to purchase a general obligation bond?

(A) Increasing assessments of property taxes

(B) Increasing municipal operating expenses

(C) Rising defaults on property taxes

(D) None of the above

143. Under MSRB rules, who approves advertising materials prior to their use?

(A) Legal counsel

(B) General securities principal

(C) MSRB

(D) Municipal securities principal

144. Under MSRB rules, which of the following is NOT considered to be an advertisement?

(A) Final official statement

(B) Offering circular

(C) Market letter

(D) Research report

145. Under MSRB rules, municipal securities dealers are allowed to use which of the following quotes?

  I. Indications of interest

 II. Nominal quotes

III. Bona fide bids and offers

IV. One-sided markets

(A) I and II

(B) II, III, and IV

(C) I, III, and IV

(D) I, II, III, and IV

146. Municipal bond GO issues are
  I. issued by the federal government and interest received is exempt from state tax
  II. exempt from registration with the SEC
  III. backed mostly by property taxes
  IV. issued to fund revenue-producing facilities

  (A) I and II
  (B) II and III
  (C) III and IV
  (D) I and IV

147. Which of the following securities are short-term municipal notes?
  I. BANs
  II. AONs
  III. RANs
  IV. PNs

  (A) I, II, and III
  (B) II, III, and IV
  (C) I, III, and IV
  (D) I, II, and IV

148. Select the true statements regarding callable municipal revenue bonds.
  I. Callable bonds appreciate more than noncallable bonds when interest rates increase.
  II. Callable bonds are usually called when market rates of interest decline.
  III. Callable bonds usually have higher coupon yields than noncallable bonds.
  IV. Callable bonds are usually called when market rates of interest increase.

  (A) I and II
  (B) I, II, and III
  (C) II and III
  (D) III and IV

149. Which of the following backs an IDR bond?
  (A) A corporate guarantor only
  (B) The local municipality if the corporate guarantor cannot meet its debt obligations
  (C) The state government in which the facility is located
  (D) None of the above

CHAPTER 4

Margin Accounts and Long and Short Investments

150. To open a margin account at an NYSE member firm, which of the following people need the employer's authorization?

(A) An employee of the NYSE
(B) An employee of another NYSE member firm
(C) A bank teller
(D) All of the above

151. An investor has a margin account with a long value of $50,000 and a debit balance of $30,000. If the investor sells 100 shares of a stock in the account at 10, how much money can he or she withdraw from the account?

(A) $1,000
(B) $500
(C) $250
(D) $0

152. Investor A has an SMA of $5,000 in a margin account. What is the investor's buying power in this account?

(A) $10,000
(B) $7,500
(C) $5,000
(D) $2,500

Questions 153–159 are based on the following information:

- Regulation T = 50 percent
- A customer's margin account contains the following securities:
  - 100 shares Intel trading at $25 per share
  - 100 shares Pepsi trading at $60 per share
  - 100 shares Exelon trading at $45 per share
  - 100 shares Exxon Mobil trading at $80 per share
- Total market value = $21,000
- Debit balance = $8,000

153. What is the customer's excess equity in the account?

    (A) $13,000
    (B) $10,500
    (C) $2,500
    (D) $0

154. What is the buying power in the account?

    (A) $10,500
    (B) $5,000
    (C) $2,500
    (D) $1,250

155. If the customer wants to buy 100 shares of Chesapeake Energy at $25 per share, what is the amount of money this investor must add to the account?

    (A) $5,000
    (B) $2,500
    (C) $1,250
    (D) $0

156. Instead of purchasing shares of Chesapeake Energy, the investor decides to purchase 100 shares of Chevron at $100 per share. How much money would the investor have to deposit in the account?

    (A) $10,000
    (B) $5,000
    (C) $2,500
    (D) $0

157. Instead of depositing cash into the account, the investor deposits securities to meet the margin call. What amount of securities must be deposited?

(A) $10,000
(B) $5,000
(C) $2,500
(D) $1,000

158. If the investor decides to deposit cash into the account for question 155, when is the cash due in the account?

(A) On the next business day after the trade
(B) Three days after the trade
(C) No later than the fifth business day after the trade
(D) No later than the sixth business day after the trade

159. If the investor does NOT make the cash payments or deposit securities for the trades in this margin account, which of the following options is open to the brokerage firm that holds the account?

(A) Restrict the account for 30 days.
(B) Lend the money to the investor.
(C) Put a hold on the account for 90 days.
(D) Liquidate the trades in the account.

160. If an investor sells short 100 shares of Freeport McMoran at $40 per share and the stock goes up to $45, how much is the restriction on the account?

(A) $2,250
(B) $1,500
(C) $750
(D) $500

161. An investor purchased 200 shares of McDonald's at $75 per share in a margin account. If McDonald's is currently trading at $90 per share, what is the investor's SMA?

(A) $1,500
(B) $2,000
(C) $2,500
(D) $3,000

162. An investor opens a margin account and sells short 100 shares of XYZ stock at $1 per share. What is the investor's margin requirement?
    (A) $50
    (B) $100
    (C) $2,000
    (D) $5,000

163. An investor has a margin account showing the following balances:
    - Long market value: $50,000
    - Debit balance: $14,000
    - Short market value: $16,000
    - Credit balance: $31,000

    What is the investor's equity in the account?
    (A) $15,000
    (B) $35,000
    (C) $51,000
    (D) $67,000

164. Which of the following is NOT included in a standard margin agreement?
    (A) The right to sell off securities to cover the dealer's debt
    (B) Authorization for the RR to trade on the account
    (C) A pledge by the investor of his or her securities to the brokerage firm
    (D) The broker/dealer's authorization to pledge margined securities

165. An investor has a margin account with a market value of $31,000 and a debit balance of $18,000. Which of the following statements is true?
    (A) The account is currently not restricted.
    (B) The account is currently restricted by $2,500.
    (C) The minimum maintenance equity is $10,000.
    (D) The investor can withdraw up to $2,500 from the account.

166. To open a margin account, an investor signs a loan consent agreement, hypothecation agreement, and credit agreement. Which of the following statements is false?
    (A) The investor pays interest on the debit balance in the account.
    (B) The debit balance fluctuates daily with the fluctuations in market value of the securities held in the account.
    (C) All the long securities in the account are held in street name.
    (D) Some of the securities may be pledged as collateral for the loans on the account.

167. An investor has a long margin account with the following balances:

1,000 shares FCX	$35,000
200 shares MCD	$18,000
500 shares EXC	$20,000
Total	$73,000
Debit balance	$36,000

How much can the brokerage firm rehypothecate from this account based on the current market value of the securities?

(A) $50,400
(B) $36,000
(C) $18,000
(D) None of the above

168. An investor has a margin account with stocks with a current worth of $60,000, and a debit balance of $25,000. How much of the investor's securities can the brokerage firm lend to itself?

(A) $25,000
(B) $35,000
(C) $60,000
(D) $84,000

169. Which of the following statements is true regarding a frozen account?

(A) The investor must deposit the cash for each transaction by the settlement date.
(B) The investor may not buy or sell securities under any circumstances.
(C) The investor may sell securities but cannot purchase securities.
(D) The investor must deposit the total cash price before the execution of any order.

170. Who determines the credit policies for a member firm?

(A) Federal Reserve Bank
(B) SEC
(C) The firm's top management
(D) NYSE

171. In a newly opened margin account, an investor purchases $100,000 of municipal bonds at a price of $110 and $100,000 of U.S. government bonds at a price of $105, with a maturity of 20 years. What is the minimum amount the investor is required to deposit?

(A) $107,500
(B) $100,000
(C) $ 22,800
(D) $ 13,000

172. When reviewing a firm's investor's statements, it was discovered that one investor had consistently paid late by five days for purchases in the investor's account. Which of the following statements is correct concerning this investor's account?

(A) This situation is acceptable if the investor has sufficient personal assets on each of the settlement dates.
(B) Late payments are acceptable if the securities purchased were not listed on the NYSE.
(C) The firm must determine whether extensions had been obtained under Regulation T.
(D) None of the above

173. When can a broker overlook an amount due in a client's account under Regulation T?

(A) When the amount due is less than $1,000 in a cash account.
(B) If the value of a trade is less than $1,000.
(C) If the client places a written request to overlook the amount due.
(D) Under no circumstances can an amount due be overlooked.

174. An investor has a short margin account with a credit balance of $4,600 and an SMV of $3,500. How much excess equity does this investor have in his or her account?

(A) None
(B) $650 restricted
(C) $1,100
(D) $1,750

175. An investor has a margin account with $45,000 market value and a debit balance of $17,000. If the investor would like to buy an additional $25,000 of stock in this account, how much must this investor deposit?

(A) $12,500
(B) $7,000
(C) $5,500
(D) $0

CHAPTER 5

Options

176. Which of the following investors would receive a dividend if the option was exercised prior to the ex-dividend date?
  I. The writer of a call option
  II. The holder of a call option
  III. The writer of a put option
  IV. The holder of a put option

  (A) I and II
  (B) II and III
  (C) III and IV
  (D) I and IV

177. An investor sells short 300 shares of AAPL stock at $360 per share. If the market price of AAPL stock declines to $330 per share, what should this investor do to protect his or her profit?

  (A) Buy three AAPL calls.
  (B) Buy three AAPL puts.
  (C) Sell three AAPL calls.
  (D) Sell three AAPL puts.

178. Which statement is correct concerning the last time an investor can trade a listed option?

  (A) 4:00 P.M. EST on the third Friday of the expiration month
  (B) 5:00 P.M. CST on the third Friday of the expiration month
  (C) 5:30 P.M. EST on the third Friday of the expiration month
  (D) 11:59 P.M. EST on the Saturday after the third Friday of the expiration month

179. A broker wants to attract new clients to his or her options section of the brokerage firm. What information should the broker's advertisements include regarding the broker's past recommendations?

(A) A list of all the money-making option recommendations made by the firm for the past year

(B) A list of all the option recommendations made by the firm for the past year

(C) A list disclosing all straddle positions held by the firm in the past year

(D) A list disclosing all security recommendations made by the firm for the past year

180. An investor is long 1 MMM Jul 100 put for 8 and is also short 1 MMM Jul 90 put for 3. How could the investor profit from this position?

  I. The options expire without being exercised.

  II. The options are exercised.

  III. The difference in the premiums widens.

  IV. The difference in the premiums narrows.

(A) I and III

(B) I and IV

(C) II and III

(D) II and IV

181. An investor buys 1 POT Jun 70 call at 6 when the market price is $70 per share. The stock price goes up to $86 when the investor exercises the contract. What are the tax consequences for this investor?

(A) The cost basis of POT stock is $70 per share.

(B) The investor has a gain of $600.

(C) The cost basis of POT stock is $76 per share.

(D) The investor has a loss of $600.

182. Microsoft stock is trading at $28 per share. Which of the following options are "in the money"?

  I. MSFT Jun 20 calls

  II. MSFT Jun 20 puts

  III. MSFT Jun 30 calls

  IV. MSFT Jun 30 puts

(A) I and II

(B) I and IV

(C) II and III

(D) III and IV

183. An investor buys one MRK Jun 40 put at 6 and sells one MRK Jun 35 put at 1. Which best describes the investor's position?

(A) Debit-bearish
(B) Credit-bearish
(C) Debit-bullish
(D) Credit-bullish

184. Which of the following positions has been created by an investor with the following two options?

- Write 1 XYZ Jun 55 put at 5
- Short 1 XYZ Jun 60 call at 4

(A) Credit spread
(B) Debit spread
(C) Short straddle
(D) Short combination

185. Who decides which securities will have options and who is the guarantor of all listed options?

(A) OCD
(B) OCC
(C) CBOE
(D) NYSE

186. A company that sells merchandise to a European company is concerned about receiving payment in Euros in two months. What would you advise the company to do to hedge its currency exposure?

(A) Buy U.S. dollar calls.
(B) Buy Euro calls.
(C) Buy U.S. dollar puts.
(D) Buy Euro puts.

187. Which of the following options contains the greatest risk?

(A) Long a call
(B) Long a put
(C) Writing a naked (uncovered) call
(D) Writing a naked put

188. A brokerage firm approves an options account for an investor, who initiates option positions. After 15 days, the brokerage firm has not received the option agreement from the investor. What action should the brokerage firm take?

(A) No specific action is required.
(B) The account must be frozen.
(C) No new option positions should be accepted.
(D) Existing option positions must be closed out.

189. Which of the following changes the strike price of a listed option?
   I. 2-for-1 stock split
  II. 4-for-1 stock split
 III. 5 percent stock dividend
  IV. $0.45 cash dividend

(A) I and IV
(B) III and IV
(C) I, II, and III
(D) II, III, and IV

190. An investor bought 200 shares of XYZ at $45 per share and then bought 2 XYZ Jun 40 puts for 4 each. If XYZ is currently trading at $48 per share, at what market price will this investor break even?

(A) $41
(B) $44
(C) $49
(D) $53

191. When do stock index options expire?

(A) Annually
(B) Quarterly
(C) Monthly
(D) Weekly

192. What is the investor's position with regard to his or her account?
   • Bought 1 XYZ Jun 20 put
   • Bought 1 XYZ Jun 30 call

(A) Short combination
(B) Long combination
(C) Short straddle
(D) Long straddle

193. What is the most likely reason an investor is prompted to write covered call options?

(A) To assist the investor in maximizing profits on long securities
(B) To increase the yield on the investor's portfolio
(C) To allow the investor to buy the shares at a discount when stock prices decline
(D) To maximize profits in the event of a bear market

194. An investor buys 1 XYZ Jun 40 call at 4 and sells 1 XYZ Jun 50 call at 2. What is the investor's maximum potential gain?

(A) $200
(B) $400
(C) $600
(D) $800

195. If the market price of the underlying stock is the same as the exercise price of an option at expiration, which of the following option positions would result in a profit?

(A) Short call
(B) Long call
(C) Long put
(D) Long combination

Questions 196–198 are based on the following information:

An investor writes 5 XYZ Jun 30 puts at 3 when the stock is trading at $32 per share, and the investor has no other positions in the stock.

196. What is the investor's maximum possible loss?

(A) $1,500
(B) $15,000
(C) $13,500
(D) Cannot be determined

197. What is the investor's maximum possible gain?

(A) $15,000
(B) $13,500
(C) $1,500
(D) Cannot be determined

198. If the stock of XYZ rises to $50 per share, and the investor purchases the options for $0.15 to close the position, what is the gain?

(A) $15,000
(B) $14,925
(C) $1,500
(D) $1,425

199. An investor buys 100 shares of XYZ at $40 per share and a few days later sells 1 XYZ Oct 45 call at 3. If the investor decides to sell the stock at $45 and closes out the option at 4, what is this investor's gain or loss?

(A) $400
(B) $500
(C) $600
(D) $700

200. An investor purchases 1 XYZ Jun 30 call at 5 and 1 XYZ Jun 25 put at 3. At expiration the stock increases to $27 and the investor does not exercise either option. What is the investor's gain or loss?

(A) $200 loss
(B) $800 loss
(C) $200 gain
(D) $800 gain

201. In which of the following situations would an investor face the potential for unlimited losses?

(A) Buy a call option and short the stock.
(B) Sell a call option and take a long position in the stock.
(C) Sell a put option and short the stock.
(D) Sell a put option and take a long position in the stock.

202. Which is NOT an advantage of purchasing a put option as compared to selling short a stock?

(A) The investor faces a limited maximum loss potential.
(B) The investor is not required to pay the dividend payments on the borrowed stock.
(C) The investor can hold interest in the same amount of securities with less expense.
(D) There is no loss on the time value as the option is held.

Question 203 is based on the following table:

XYZ	Strike	Jun	Sept	Dec
40.25	30	11	13	15
40.25	30p	0.10	0.50	1.25
40.25	40	1.50	3	4.50
40.25	40p	1.35	2.50	4

203. An investor buys an XYZ Dec 40 put and writes an XYZ Dec 30 put. What is the maximum gain for this investor?

(A) $275
(B) $625
(C) $725
(D) $1,275

204. An investor writes an uncovered call option, which expires unexercised. What are the tax consequences for this investor?

(A) The investor has ordinary income equal to the premium recognized at expiration.
(B) The investor has a capital gain equal to the premium recognized at expiration.
(C) The investor has a capital loss equal to the premium recognized at expiration.
(D) The investor has ordinary losses equal to the premium recognized at expiration.

205. If the market price of a stock and the exercise price is the same and remains that way, which of the following situations would be profitable?

I. The buyer of an at-the-money call
II. The buyer of an at-the-money put
III. The seller of an at-the-money call
IV. The seller of an at-the-money straddle

(A) I and II
(B) III and IV
(C) I and III
(D) II and IV

206. An investor has a portfolio that consists of majority holdings in bonds and preferred stocks. Which of the following is the best option strategy to protect against the decline in the prices of bonds and preferred stocks?

(A) Buy interest rate calls.
(B) Buy interest rate puts.
(C) Buy index option puts.
(D) Buy index option calls.

207. An investor writes five naked puts on XYZ stock. What is the maximum loss that this investor can incur?

(A) The amount of the premium
(B) (Strike price + the premium) × 100 shares × 5 options
(C) (Strike price − the premium) × 100 shares × 5 options
(D) Unlimited

208. An investor buys 1 XYZ Jan 50 put at 6 and also purchases 100 shares of XYZ at $55 per share. What is the investor's breakeven point?

(A) $44
(B) $49
(C) $56
(D) $61

Question 209 is based on the following table:

	Bid	Offer
XYZ Jun 40 call	3	3.25
XYZ Jun 40 put	2	2.25
XYZ Jun 50 call	1	1.25
XYZ Jun 50 put	5	6

209. If an investor created a debit call spread, how much would the investor have to pay?

(A) $125
(B) $175
(C) $200
(D) $225

210. If interest rates are expected to increase, which of the following option strategies would be profitable?

    I. Buy Treasury bond calls.

   II. Buy Treasury bond puts.

 III. Sell Treasury bond calls.

 IV. Sell Treasury bond puts.

    (A) I and II

    (B) II and III

    (C) I and IV

    (D) II and IV

Questions 211–213 are based on the following information:

An investor purchases an XYZ Jun 90 call for 11 and sells an XYZ Jun 100 call for 5 when the stock is trading at $95 per share.

211. How much money must the investor deposit to meet the margin requirement?

    (A) $600

    (B) $1,000

    (C) $1,100

    (D) $1,600

212. Below what stock price would this investor lose money if the option spread is held until expiration?

    (A) $95

    (B) $96

    (C) $101

    (D) $105

213. What is the investor's maximum possible gain in this situation?

    (A) $400

    (B) $1,000

    (C) $1,400

    (D) $1,600

214. An exporter is paid in British pounds for purchases. If the exporter wants to protect against a fall in value of British pounds, the exporter should

    (A) sell calls

    (B) buy calls

    (C) sell puts

    (D) buy puts

Questions 215–218 are based on the following information:

An investor purchases 1 XYZ Aug 50 call for 5 and purchases 1 XYZ Aug 50 put for 3 when the stock is trading at $53 per share.

215. What is this investor's expectations about the price of XYZ stock before the August expiration?

(A) Rising prices
(B) Declining prices
(C) Stable prices
(D) Volatility in prices and uncertainty in direction

216. What are the breakeven points for this investor's position?

I. $42
II. $45
III. $53
IV. $58

(A) I only
(B) III only
(C) I and IV
(D) II and III

217. What is the maximum possible gain for this investor?

(A) $800
(B) $1,600
(C) $49,200
(D) Unlimited

218. What is the maximum possible loss for this investor?

(A) $300
(B) $500
(C) $800
(D) Unlimited

219. An investor buys an OEX CAPS360 call option for 6. What price would OEX have to pass before automatic execution?

(A) $330
(B) $366
(C) $390
(D) $396

220. Which of the following strategies provides an investor with limited upside protection?

(A) Buy puts
(B) Buy limit orders
(C) Write uncovered call options
(D) Stop orders to sell

Questions 221–223 are based on the following information:

An investor buys 1 XYZ Aug 35 put at 6 and writes 1 XYZ Aug 25 put at 3 when the stock price is trading at $31 per share.

221. What is the breakeven point for this investor?

(A) $32
(B) $28
(C) $26
(D) $22

222. What is the maximum possible gain for this investor?

(A) $300
(B) $400
(C) $700
(D) Unlimited

223. If the stock price trades at $38 at the August expiration, what is the gain or loss for this investor?

(A) $300 gain
(B) $300 loss
(C) $600 gain
(D) $600 loss

224. What is the sequential order for placing options transactions for an investor's first options trade with you?

I. The investor is sent an ODD.
II. The investor sends in an OAA.
III. The ROP approves the account.
IV. The transaction is executed.

(A) I, III, IV, II
(B) II, III, I, IV
(C) I, III, II, IV
(D) III, I, IV, II

225. An investor owns 100 shares of XYZ, which were purchased at $60 per share. When the stock trades at $58 per share, the investor decides to write 1 XYZ Aug 65 call at 4. What is the investor's maximum potential loss?

(A) $100
(B) $5,600
(C) $6,100
(D) $6,900

226. An investor owns shares of XYZ Corp for 11 months. Which of the following strategies would affect the investor's holding period on the stock?

   I. Buying XYZ call options
  II. Buying XYZ put options
 III. Selling XYZ put options
  IV. Selling XYZ stock short against the box

(A) I and II
(B) II and IV
(C) III and IV
(D) None of the above

227. An investor purchases 5 XYZ Aug 30 calls at 3. When do these options expire?

(A) On the third Friday in August
(B) On the third Saturday in August
(C) On the Saturday following the third Friday in August
(D) On the last Friday of August

228. An investor purchases 1 XYZ Aug 30 call at 7 when the stock is trading at $35.25. What is the time value of the XYZ Aug 30 calls?

(A) $700
(B) $525
(C) $175
(D) $0

229. An investor writes an uncovered XYZ Jan 35 put for 4 when stock of XYZ is trading at $38 per share. If the put option is exercised when the stock is trading at $32 per share in December, what are the tax consequences for the investor who wrote the put option?

(A) The cost basis is $31 per share in XYZ stock.
(B) There is a $300 loss.
(C) There is a $300 gain.
(D) There is a $500 loss.

230. Which of the following will NOT change the number of shares outstanding when exercised?

(A) Convertible bonds
(B) Warrants
(C) Rights
(D) Options

231. An investor writes 3 Dec OEX (S&P 100) 125 calls at 3. The options are exercised when the S&P index closes at 131. What is this investor's gain or loss?

(A) $1,800
(B) $900
(C) $600
(D) $300

232. Which of the following positions represents the greatest dollar risk?

(A) Long stock and short call
(B) Short stock and long call
(C) Long stock and long put
(D) Short stock and short put

Questions 233–235 are based on the following information:

An investor writes 1 XYZ Jun 35 put for 8 and buys 1 XYZ Jun 25 put for 4 when the stock of XYZ is trading at $29 per share.

233. Which one of the following does NOT describe the spread?

(A) Money
(B) Bull
(C) Credit
(D) Diagonal

234. At what price should the stock of XYZ be at expiration to give the investor the largest gain?

(A) $35
(B) $31
(C) $29
(D) $25

235. What is the breakeven point for this investor at expiration?

(A) $35
(B) $31
(C) $29
(D) $27

Questions 236–238 are based on the following information:

An investor purchased 100 shares of XYZ at $57 per share and at the same time purchased 1 XYZ Jun 60 put at 7.

236. What is the maximum possible loss on this position prior to expiration?

(A) $300
(B) $700
(C) $1,000
(D) Unlimited

237. What is the breakeven point on the stock before expiration?

(A) $50
(B) $53
(C) $64
(D) $67

238. What is the maximum gain if the stock is trading at $67 at expiration?

(A) $0
(B) $300
(C) $700
(D) $1,000

239. An investor buys 6 XYZ Jun 60 calls for 7 when the stock is trading at $78. Subsequently, the company announces a 3-for-2 split. What is this investor's position after the split takes effect?

(A) 9 XYZ Jun 40 calls
(B) 4 XYZ Jun 90 calls
(C) 6 XYZ Jun 40 calls
(D) 9 XYZ Jun 60 calls

240. A put option is in-the-money when the market price of the stock is

(A) higher than the strike price
(B) lower than the strike price
(C) higher than the strike price minus the premium
(D) lower than the strike price minus the premium

241. An investor sells the stock of ABC Company. Which of the following actions, if done within the 30-day period of selling the stock, would prevent the investor from taking the tax loss deduction?

  I. Purchase an ABC put option.
 II. Purchase an ABC call option.
III. Purchase ABC convertible bonds.
IV. Purchase ABC common stock.

(A) I and III
(B) I, III, and IV
(C) II, III, and IV
(D) II and IV

242. An investor expects the stock price of XYZ to appreciate and has no position in the stock. What actions should the investor take to profit from his or her expectations about the stock?

  I. Purchase XYZ call options.
 II. Purchase XYZ put options.
III. Sell XYZ call options.
IV. Sell XYZ put options.

(A) I and IV
(B) II and III
(C) II and IV
(D) I and III

243. An investor expects the stock price of XYZ to decline and has no position in the stock. What actions should the investor take to profit from his or her expectations on the stock?

  I. Purchase XYZ call options.
 II. Purchase XYZ put options.
III. Sell XYZ call options.
IV. Sell XYZ put options.

(A) I and IV
(B) II and III
(C) II and IV
(D) I and III

Questions 244–247 are based on the following information:

An investor buys 200 shares XYZ at $34 per share and then sells 2 XYZ Jun 35 calls for 2.

244. What is this investor's maximum possible gain?
  (A) $200
  (B) $400
  (C) $600
  (D) Unlimited

245. What is this investor's maximum possible loss?
  (A) $6,000
  (B) $6,400
  (C) $7,200
  (D) Unlimited

246. What is this investor's breakeven point?
  (A) $32
  (B) $33
  (C) $35
  (D) $36

247. At expiration, the stock is trading at $34.50 and the investor sells the shares and closes out the option at its intrinsic value. What is this investor's gain or loss?
  (A) $100 gain
  (B) $500 gain
  (C) $300 loss
  (D) $100 loss

248. In which situations would an uncovered call option seller profit?
   I. The price of the underlying stock decreases.
  II. The price of the underlying stock increases.
 III. The option is exercised.
  IV. The option expires.
  (A) II and IV
  (B) II and III
  (C) I only
  (D) I and IV

249. What is the loan value of a call option held in a margin account?

(A) Same as the FRB's initial margin requirement for listed stocks
(B) 50 percent
(C) 25 percent
(D) 0 percent

250. How would the premium costs on a LEAP option compare with the premium costs on a traditional option on the same security with the same strike price?

(A) The premiums will be approximately the same.
(B) The premium for the traditional option will be greater than the LEAP option premium.
(C) The premium for the LEAP option will be greater than the traditional option premium.
(D) It is impossible to make any of the above generalizations.

251. When an option holder is only permitted to exercise the contract at expiration, the option is referred to as

(A) American style
(B) Nordic style
(C) European style
(D) Asian style

252. Which of the following is NOT true of exchange-traded options?

(A) They are adjusted for cash dividends.
(B) They are adjusted for stock dividends.
(C) They are adjusted for stock splits.
(D) They are adjusted for reverse splits.

253. Under what circumstances is the holder of a listed call option entitled to receive a dividend payable on the underlying stock?

(A) Never
(B) Always
(C) Only if the holder submits an exercise notice to the OCC after the ex-dividend date
(D) Only if the holder submits an exercise notice to the OCC before the ex-dividend date

254. Which of the following is NOT set by the Options Clearing Corporation for listed options?

(A) Contract size
(B) Premium amount
(C) Strike price
(D) Expiration

255. How is settlement made when index options are exercised?

(A) Cash
(B) Delivery of the underlying securities
(C) Delivery of a futures contract
(D) Any of the above

256. Which of the following contracts on foreign currencies are represented by options traded on the Philadelphia Stock Exchange?

I. Euros
II. Swiss francs
III. British pounds
IV. Australian dollars

(A) I and II
(B) I and III
(C) I, II, and III
(D) I, II, III, and IV

CHAPTER 6

Investment Companies

257. An investor would like to purchase $20,000 of an international growth stock fund. How many shares can this investor purchase if the NAV is $10.00, the POP is $10.85, and the sales charge can be found in the following table?

Breakpoint	Sales Charge %
$0–$9,999	8%
$10,000–$19,999	7%
$20,000–$29,999	6%
$30,000–$39,999	5%
$40,000 and up	4%

(A) 1,843.32
(B) 1,879.70
(C) 1,886.79
(D) 2,000.00

258. Based on the NAV and POP, which one of the following is a closed-end fund?

(A) NAV $9, POP $9.15
(B) NAV $10, POP $10.99
(C) NAV $22, POP $22.90
(D) NAV $5.50, POP $5.75

259. An investor is looking for recommendations on municipal bond funds. Which of the following would be important to this investor?

(A) The investor's tax bracket
(B) The investor's legal residence
(C) The investor's asset allocation
(D) All of the above

260. The NAV of a mutual fund is affected by

(A) depreciation
(B) amortization
(C) appreciation
(D) annualization

261. With regard to mutual fund investing, which of the following statements best describe(s) dollar cost averaging?

(A) Purchasing a fixed number of shares periodically
(B) Investing a fixed dollar amount into the same investment periodically
(C) Maintaining a fixed dollar amount invested in mutual funds
(D) All of the above

262. Which type of mutual fund typically invests in both bonds and equities?

(A) Growth funds
(B) Dual purpose funds
(C) Technology funds
(D) Balanced funds

263. An open-end mutual fund with a maximum sales charge of 7.5 percent has a bid and offer quote of $10.00 - $10.81. If the sales charge is reduced to 6 percent for purchases of $40,000 to $54,999, how many shares would an investor get by investing $50,000?

(A) 4,625.35
(B) 4,699.25
(C) 4,716.98
(D) 5,000

264. Which of the following are true of closed-end funds but NOT true of open-end funds?

  I. Shares trade above, below, or at net asset values.
 II. Shares are traded on the stock exchanges.
III. New shares are constantly being issued.
IV. Investors may redeem their shares.

(A) I and II
(B) III and IV
(C) I, II, and IV
(D) I, II, III, and IV

265. A new investor is seeking your advice with regard to selecting mutual funds to invest in. Which is the most important factor you would advise the investor to consider when choosing funds?

(A) 12(b)1 fees
(B) Management fees
(C) Investment objectives
(D) Sales charges

266. The operating fees of a mutual fund divided by the fund's average net asset value is referred to as the

(A) P/E ratio
(B) quick ratio
(C) current ratio
(D) expense ratio

Questions 267–269 are based on the following table:

Fund Change	Investment Objectives	NAV	Offer Price	NAV
Vanguard Group				
STAR	S&B	13.39	NL	+0.07
GNMA	BND	10.53	NL	+0.02
Westcore				
GNMA	BND	16.45	17.23	+0.02
ST Govt	BST	15.87	16.19	

267. Which of the following funds do NOT have a sales charge?
  I. The Vanguard Group's STAR fund
  II. The Vanguard Group's GNMA fund
  III. Westcore's GNMA fund
  IV. Westcore's ST Govt. fund

(A) I and II
(B) II and III
(C) III and IV
(D) I and IV

268. Which of the four funds is a balanced fund?

(A) The Vanguard Group's STAR fund
(B) The Vanguard Group's GNMA fund
(C) Westcore's GNMA fund
(D) Westcore's ST Govt. fund

269. Which of the funds has the highest sales charge?

    (A) The Vanguard Group's STAR fund
    (B) The Vanguard Group's GNMA fund
    (C) Westcore's GNMA fund
    (D) Westcore's ST Govt. fund

270. Which of the following statements about mutual funds and variable annuities are false?

    I. At death, property passes to the estate of the owner.
    II. They are regulated by the Investment Company Act of 1940.
    III. Investment income and capital gains realized by the portfolio are passed on to the owners to report on their tax returns.

    (A) I and III
    (B) I and II
    (C) II and III
    (D) I, II, and III

271. A new open-end mutual fund company wants to advertise with a prospectus, which must

    I. have a statement indicating that the fund is not monitored by a government body
    II. include only statements that are true
    III. include a disclaimer that past performance may not be indicative of future performance
    IV. omit facts that would confuse investors

    (A) I, II, III, and IV
    (B) I, II, and III
    (C) I, III, and IV
    (D) I, III, and IV

272. The POP of a mutual fund is

    (A) net asset value $\times$ sales charge
    (B) net asset value $-$ sales charge
    (C) net asset value $+$ sales charge
    (D) net asset value/sales charge

273. When considering the suitability of investing in a variable annuity, what is the most important factor for an RR to mention to a potential investor?

    (A) Variable annuities have a sales charge.
    (B) Variable annuities may charge management fees.
    (C) The investor's deposits may decrease.
    (D) Payments made to the investor may decrease.

274. Which of the following is NOT true regarding a no-load mutual fund?
(A) Investors can buy shares of this fund through broker-dealers.
(B) Investors can sell their shares at any time.
(C) The fund can charge 12(b)1 fees and other management fees.
(D) Investors in the fund do not pay sales charges.

275. Which of the following statements are true with regard to investment company advertisements used by your brokerage firm?
  I. They must be filed with FINRA within 10 days of first use.
  II. They must be approved by FINRA and then filed with FINRA before use.
  III. They must be approved by the SEC and then filed with them before use.
  IV. They must be approved by a principal of the brokerage firm in writing before first use.
(A) I and IV
(B) II and III
(C) I and II
(D) III and IV

276. Which statement is true about variable annuities during the annuity period?
(A) The annuity unit value is fixed, but the number of annuity units varies.
(B) The annuity value per unit is fixed, and the number of accumulation units is fixed.
(C) The annuity unit value varies, but the number of annuity units is fixed.
(D) The assumed interest rate varies, and the number of annuity units also varies.

277. When do accumulation units in a variable annuity get converted into annuity units?
(A) When the value of the investment exceeds $200,000
(B) When the insurance company releases the funds
(C) When the trust is dissolved
(D) When the investor begins to receive payments

278. The ex-dividend date for mutual funds is

    (A) three business days prior to the record date
    (B) determined by the mutual fund sponsor
    (C) two business days after the record date
    (D) the last day of each month

279. Which of the following descriptions are true of variable annuities?

    I. Variable dollar premiums acquiring a fixed number of accumulation units
    II. Fixed dollar investments acquiring a variable number of accumulation units
    III. Fixed number of annuity units giving payouts that vary in amount
    IV. Variable number of annuity units giving fixed payout amounts

    (A) I and II
    (B) I and III
    (C) II and III
    (D) II and IV

280. An investor in a high marginal tax bracket is interested in investing to obtain high levels of income while minimizing tax liability. Which type of investment would you suggest?

    (A) Blue-chip stock fund
    (B) Money market fund
    (C) Municipal bond fund
    (D) Zero-coupon bond fund

281. An investor invests $1,000 every month for four months in a no-load blue-chip fund. If the NAV for each month is shown below, what is the average cost per share?

Month 1 $30
Month 2 $40
Month 3 $30
Month 4 $40

    (A) $32
    (B) $34.31
    (C) $35
    (D) $38.3

282. Which of the following statements is/are NOT true of REITs?

  I. They pass off income and write-offs to investors to avoid being taxed as a corporation.

  II. At least 90 percent of the net income received by the REIT is distributed to investors to avoid being taxed as a corporation.

  III. The REIT is a trust that invests in real estate–related projects.

  IV. At least 75 percent of the income comes from real estate–related activities in order to qualify to not be taxed as a corporation.

  (A) I only
  (B) I and IV
  (C) II and IV
  (D) I and II

283. Which of the following statements is NOT true of a unit investment trust (UIT)?

  (A) A registered investment company purchases a fixed portfolio of income-producing securities and holds them in trust.
  (B) The investment company issues shares that represent investors' interest in the trust.
  (C) The UIT pays investment advisor fees to its investment advisors who actively manage the assets of the trust.
  (D) Income in the form of interest or dividends and capital gains are passed on to investors.

284. An investor in a variable annuity is making periodic payments to the annuity. During the accumulation stage the investor would expect to receive which form of distribution from the annuity?

  (A) Interest
  (B) Dividends
  (C) Capital gains
  (D) None of the above

285. According to the Internal Revenue Service, a REIT must distribute what percentage of its net income to shareholders?

  (A) 60 percent
  (B) 75 percent
  (C) 90 percent
  (D) 100 percent

286. When a bank or trust company acts as a custodian for a mutual fund it

(A) protects the mutual fund's assets physically
(B) issues and redeems fund shares
(C) guarantees investors' gains and losses on their investments in the fund
(D) advises fund managers on the choice of investments to purchase for the fund

287. Which of the following statements about no-load funds are true?

I. They cannot charge 12(b)1 fees.
II. They can charge redemption or liquidation fees when investors sell shares.
III. If investors do not invest the minimum required amount, the fund can charge sales charges up to 5 percent.
IV. Shares are issued and redeemed directly through and from the mutual fund company.

(A) I and III
(B) II and IV
(C) I, II, and IV
(D) II, III, and IV

288. If a mutual fund wants to change its investment objective from a value fund to a growth fund, the investment company must get approval from

(A) a majority of the shareholders
(B) FINRA
(C) SEC
(D) All of the above

289. What is the minimum net worth that a registered investment company must have under the 1940 Investment Company Act?

(A) $25,000
(B) $50,000
(C) $100,000
(D) $150,000

290. A mutual fund has a 5 percent load and a 2 percent redemption fee. The quote for the fund is $7.04 - $7.41. If a shareholder wants to sell shares, what share price will the investor receive?

(A) $7.41
(B) $7.26
(C) $7.04
(D) $6.90

291. Which of the following statements best describes a reinvestment plan for a load mutual fund?

(A) Dividends and capital gains distributions from the fund are not taxed at the federal level.

(B) Investors in the fund can make regular purchases of additional shares at the net asset value price.

(C) Any distributions in the form of income, dividends, and capital gains are automatically reinvested in new shares of the fund.

(D) Investors in the fund must agree to make regular investments in the fund.

292. Up to what length of time may a mutual fund letter of intent be predated?

(A) 3 days

(B) 15 days

(C) 90 days

(D) 13 months

293. Which of the following types of investment companies cannot issue long-term debt?

(A) Unit investment trust company

(B) Open-end investment company

(C) Closed-end management company

(D) All of the above

294. How often are investment companies required to issue financial statements to their shareholders?

(A) Monthly

(B) Quarterly

(C) Semiannually

(D) Annually

295. The dollar amount at which the sales charge is reduced on quantity transactions in the purchase of open-end mutual fund shares is referred to as

(A) breakpoint

(B) offer price

(C) split

(D) spread

296. Which of the following accurately defines income from an investment company?

(A) Capital gains on sales of portfolio securities
(B) Interest, dividends, and capital gains from the sales of portfolio assets
(C) Interest and dividends paid on securities in the fund's portfolio
(D) All of the above

297. Reinvestment of dividends and capital gains from investment company shares

(A) allows investors to defer federal income taxes on dividends and capital gains until shares are sold
(B) allows investors to purchase shares in the fund at discount prices
(C) allows for compounded growth in the investment account
(D) None of the above

298. Which of the following types of funds offer the potential to be purchased at a discount from its net asset value?

  I. Closed-end fund
 II. Open-end fund
III. No-load fund
IV. Contractual plan

(A) I and III
(B) I only
(C) II, III, and IV
(D) I, III, and IV

299. Net investment income from an open-end mutual fund represents

(A) net gains on the sale of portfolio securities
(B) dividends, interest, and net gains or losses on sales of securities
(C) net income from dividends and interest paid on securities held in the fund's portfolio
(D) net profit from the investment company's operations

300. The principal underwriter of an open-end investment company is called the

(A) investment counselor
(B) participating investment advisor
(C) selling group member
(D) sponsor

CHAPTER 7

Underwriting:
The Securities Act of 1933

301. A participating firm in a securities underwriting is said to be liable severally. This type of underwriting is called

(A) a firm commitment offering
(B) an Eastern account
(C) a Western account
(D) a best efforts offering

302. When new securities are offered, members of the syndicate are allowed to sell to other dealers less the reallowance. Which of the following determines the amount of the reallowance?

(A) Syndicate manager
(B) Issuing corporation
(C) SEC
(D) NYSE

303. When any unsold securities of a public offering are returned to the issuer, what is this referred to as?

(A) A firm commitment
(B) A best efforts offering
(C) All or none offering
(D) None of the above

304. Which of the following would be included in a tombstone advertisement?
   I. Where investors can obtain a prospectus
   II. An offering price
   III. A listing of syndicate members
   IV. A listing of the selling group members

   (A) I and IV
   (B) II, III, and IV
   (C) I, III, and IV
   (D) I, II, and III

305. Which of the following are NOT required on a "red herring" (preliminary prospectus)?
   I. Final offering price
   II. Issuer's financial status
   III. A statement that some items may change before the final prospectus
   IV. The effective date

   (A) I and IV
   (B) I and II
   (C) II and III
   (D) III and IV

306. Which of the following statements about Regulation A offerings is true?

   (A) Securities up to $10,000,000 can be raised within a 12-month period.
   (B) The offering is not exempt from the registration requirements of the Securities Act of 1933.
   (C) Regulation A offerings can be a private placement.
   (D) Regulation A security offerings use an offering circular in place of a prospectus.

307. An investment bank can do all of the following EXCEPT

   (A) sell securities on an agency basis
   (B) become a syndicate manager
   (C) underwrite new issues
   (D) give advice to an issuer on how to raise money

308. Which of the following bids is the best way to stabilize a new stock issue offered at 40?

I. 40
II. 39.90
III. 40.90
IV. 41

(A) I and III
(B) III and IV
(C) I and II
(D) IV only

309. An underwriter of a new offering of common stock decides to offer the issue to the public in three states. Which of the following statements are true?

I. The issuer need only register the security with the SEC and the home state of the issuer.
II. The issuer is responsible for registering the security with the SEC and also in each state in which the securities are to be sold.
III. The issuer must meet and comply with any existing blue sky requirements of all three states.
IV. The brokerage firm selling the securities need not be registered in the customer's state.

(A) I and III
(B) II and IV
(C) III and IV
(D) II and III

310. Company XYZ wants to go public and contacts Sack & Gold, an investment banking firm, to underwrite the issue. Sack & Gold forms a syndicate because the issue is large. If the public offering price is $20.50 per share, Sack & Gold will receive $19.00 per share for each share issued, the manager's fee is $0.30 per share, and the concession is $0.45 per share, what is the additional takedown?

(A) $0.75
(B) $1.05
(C) $1.20
(D) $1.50

311. Which of the following statements are true concerning securities that are sold under SEC Rule 144?
   I. Stock acquired privately must be held for one year before it is eligible for sale.
   II. If the number of shares sold is more than 1,000 or the shares are more than $20,000 in value, the SEC must be notified of the sale.
   III. The company must file regular financial data with the SEC.
   IV. The details of the sale must be reported to the SEC.

   (A) I and IV
   (B) I and II
   (C) II and III
   (D) III and IV

312. Which of the following criteria would be most important in determining which underwriter would win the competitive bidding for secured bonds of a utility company?

   (A) The refunding provision terms in the bond indenture
   (B) The highest amount received by the issuer
   (C) The lowest net interest cost to the issuer
   (D) None of the above

313. Which of the following statements is NOT true concerning the cooling-off period?

   (A) After an issuer files a registration statement with the SEC, a 10-day cooling-off period begins.
   (B) During the cooling-off period, the underwriter can get indications of interest from prospective purchasers of the securities.
   (C) Underwriters during the cooling-off period use the preliminary prospectus to obtain indications of interest from prospective investors.
   (D) Indications of interest are not binding on customers or underwriters.

314. An investor purchased shares of restricted stock, which were fully paid for and held for 18 months, and wants to sell this stock under Rule 144. There are 2,000,000 shares of the company's stock outstanding, and the trading volumes of the shares of the company during the past five weeks are as follows:

Week 1   26,000
Week 2   24,000
Week 3   28,000
Week 4   22,000
Week 5   29,000 (most recent week)

What is the maximum number of shares that this investor can sell with the Rule 144 filing?

(A) 25,800
(B) 25,750
(C) 25,000
(D) 20,000

315. Which of the following statements is/are required for an intrastate offering to qualify under Rule 147?

(A) The company must be incorporated in the state in which it is selling securities.
(B) Eighty percent of its business has to be within the state.
(C) It may sell securities only to residents of the state.
(D) All of the above

316. Which of the following statements is true regarding the public offering of securities by an underwriting syndicate?

(A) The reallowance is always greater than the selling concession.
(B) The selling concession is always greater than the underwriting spread.
(C) The underwriting spread is greater than the selling concession.
(D) The reallowance is greater than the underwriting spread.

317. In a registered public offering of 1,000,000 shares, the manager of the syndicate advises an underwriter of 50,000 shares that its retention will be 75 percent. How many shares can the underwriter sell to its own customers?

(A) 37,500 shares
(B) 12,500 shares
(C) 50,000 shares
(D) None of the above

318. Which securities are exempt from the registration requirements under the Securities Act of 1933?
  I. Securities issued by the U.S. government
  II. Public utility stocks
  III. Securities issued by banks and savings institutions
  IV. New issues of corporate securities

  (A) I and II
  (B) II and IV
  (C) I, II, and III
  (D) III and IV

319. An underwriter can cancel a proposed public offering due to an unforeseen occurrence with a provision referred to as the

  (A) fill or kill provision
  (B) market-out clause
  (C) blue sky provision
  (D) contra-market clause

320. SEC Rule 145 applies to the sale of unrestricted stock acquired as a result of

  (A) merger or acquisition
  (B) stock split
  (C) a no-sale ruling from the SEC
  (D) None of the above

321. Which of the following does NOT affect the public offering price of a new issue?

  (A) Projected dividends for the year
  (B) Anticipated earnings for the coming year
  (C) Anticipated sales growth of the issuer's products
  (D) The selling group's determination of the stock price

322. Under Rule 144, which of the following holders of unregistered stock is precluded from selling that stock?

  (A) An officer of the issuing company
  (B) A broker/dealer organization
  (C) A majority holder of the outstanding stock
  (D) None of the above

323. Which of the following statements is NOT true of a "best efforts" offering?

  (A) The investment banker acts as an agent and is paid a commission for whatever stock is sold.

  (B) The investment banker makes no guarantee for the sales of the offering.

  (C) The underwriter buys the shares from the company guaranteeing the price.

  (D) If done on "an all or none" basis, no sales are final unless the entire issue is sold.

324. In which case is an issuer most likely to ask for an investment letter from the purchaser in connection with an offering?

  (A) Closed-end fund

  (B) Issue of low-quality

  (C) Hot issue

  (D) Private placement

325. A corporation has the following capital structure: 400,000 shares of unauthorized and unissued stock and 200,000 shares that were sold to an affiliated person. Which of the following statements are true if the corporation registers a public offering of 600,000 shares?

  I. The primary offering consists of 600,000 shares.

  II. The corporation receives the entire amount of the proceeds from the offering.

  III. The primary offering consists of 400,000 shares.

  IV. The affiliated person receives one-third of the proceeds, and the corporation receives the balance of the proceeds.

  (A) I and II

  (B) II and III

  (C) III and IV

  (D) I and IV

326. In a firm commitment offering, shares that are NOT sold

  (A) are owned by the syndicate members

  (B) are given back to the issuing corporation

  (C) become Treasury stock of the issuing corporation

  (D) are returned to the issuing corporation in addition to all the shares that have been sold

327. Which of the following securities are exempt from SEC registration?
   I. Interstate offerings
   II. Variable annuities
   III. Intrastate offerings
   IV. Private placements

   (A) I and II
   (B) I and III
   (C) III and IV
   (D) II, III, and IV

328. Which of the following actions is NOT true during the cooling-off period?

   (A) Blue-skying the issue
   (B) Stabilizing the issue
   (C) Holding a due diligence meeting
   (D) Issuing the preliminary prospectus

329. If a company holds back some of its new shares for later use, this company, according to a shelf registration, can sell these shares over what period of time without having to reregister them?

   (A) 180 days
   (B) 270 days
   (C) One year
   (D) Two years

330. A company has filed a registration statement with the SEC for new shares and is currently in the cooling-off period. The lead underwriter is in the process of taking indications of interest. Which of the following statements are true regarding indications of interest?
   I. They are binding on the customer.
   II. They are binding on the underwriter.
   III. They are not binding on the underwriter.
   IV. They are not binding on the customer.

   (A) I and II
   (B) III and IV
   (C) I and III
   (D) II and IV

331. Your company is involved in underwriting municipal bonds, and the syndicate manager notifies your company that the issue is oversubscribed. How does the syndicate manager determine which orders are filled first?

(A) In the manner that the syndicate manager determines to be equitable

(B) All members' orders first

(C) As stated in the underwriter's agreement

(D) As stated in the bond indenture

332. The confirmation order sent to an investor who has purchased new GO bonds should include all of the following EXCEPT

(A) the current yield at the time of the sale

(B) the nominal yield and maturity date

(C) the settlement date

(D) the customer's name

CHAPTER 8

Exchanges:
The NYSE and NASD

333. Which of the following are NOT true of ADRs?
   I. The investor is not permitted to receive cash dividends.
   II. The investor does not receive an actual stock certificate.
   III. They are receipts for U.S. stocks that trade on foreign exchanges.
   IV. The actual shares are held in a custodial bank.

   (A) I and III
   (B) II and IV
   (C) I and II
   (D) II and III

Questions 334 and 335 are based on the following information:

Specialist's Book

XYZ Common Stock

Bid	Price	Ask
4 Merrill	26.	
8 Morgan	.15	
	.30	4 Salomon (stop)
14 Goldman	.40	
	.45	
6 Bear (stop)	.50	
	.60	12 Salomon
	.70	5 Goldman

334. What is the inside market?

   (A) 26.00 - 26.70
   (B) 26.50 - 26.7
   (C) 26.40 - 26.60
   (D) 26.00 - 26.30

335. At what price can the specialist enter a quote for his or her own inventory?

(A) 26.45
(B) Greater than 26.70
(C) Less than 26.00
(D) 26.30

336. A brokerage firm purchases 5,000 shares of XYZ common stock at $25 per share for its own inventory. A month later when the stock is quoted at $23.25–$24.00, the brokerage firm decides to sell 500 shares to one of its customers. What is the price before the markup that the brokerage firm can charge?

(A) $23.25
(B) $23.75
(C) $24.00
(D) $25.00

337. According to the "know your customer" rule, a registered representative when opening a new account for a customer should find out which of the following?

   I. Customer's investment objectives
  II. Customer's date of birth
 III. Customer's Social Security number
  IV. Customer's risk tolerance

(A) II and III
(B) I, II, and III
(C) I, III, and IV
(D) I, II, III, and IV

338. If an individual gives specific investment advice for a fee, which exams is he or she required to have passed?

(A) Series 7 and Series 66
(B) Series 63 and Series 65
(C) Series 7, Series 63, and Series 65
(D) Series 7, Series 63, Series 65, and Series 66

339. Mr. and Mrs. Smith have a joint account at your brokerage firm. Mrs. Smith asks you to sell 1,000 shares of XYZ Corporation from their joint account and to send her a check in her name only for the proceeds from the sale. As the registered representative, which of the following courses of action should you follow?

(A) Call Mr. Smith and explain the situation before you execute the transaction.

(B) Execute the trade and make sure that the check is made out to both Mr. and Mrs. Smith.

(C) Execute the trade and make sure that the check is made out to Mrs. Smith.

(D) Tell Mrs. Smith to put her request in writing before you can execute the sale.

340. Under FINRA Rule 2790, which of the following people are NOT considered "immediate family"?

   I. Father-in-law

  II. Aunt

 III. Grandfather

 IV. Sister

(A) II and III

(B) I and III

(C) I, II, and III

(D) I and IV

341. Mrs. Smith places a market order to sell 100 shares of XYZ Corporation. She is led to believe that the trade might have been traded at $25.30 per share. However, the brokerage firm notifies her that the trade was made at $25.20. Which of the following statements is true regarding this transaction?

(A) Mrs. Smith will receive $2,530 minus any commissions.

(B) Mrs. Smith will receive $2,520 minus any commissions.

(C) Mrs. Smith will receive $2,520 minus any commissions and will receive $10 from the RR.

(D) Mrs. Smith will receive $2,520 but is not liable to pay any commissions.

342. When an investor buys an OTC stock from a brokerage firm that is a market maker in the stock, the investor pays the price that

(A) includes a commission and a markup
(B) does not include a markup
(C) includes a markup
(D) includes a commission, a markup, and a special fee

343. A brokerage firm is distributing a new issue of shares, and a registered representative of the firm wants to buy shares of this new issue. Under NASD Conduct Rules, the RR may

  I. do so
 II. buy for his family
III. buy only a small allotment of the issue
IV. not do so

(A) I only
(B) II and III
(C) III only
(D) IV only

344. An investor is about to open a new cash account at your brokerage firm and wants to give trading authorization to the investor's brother. Which of the following is required for you to open an account?

  I. Joint account agreement
 II. Hypothecation agreement
III. New account form
IV. Limited power of attorney

(A) I and III
(B) II and III
(C) III and IV
(D) I, III, and IV

345. An investor decides to purchase municipal bonds through your firm. If the bonds are sold out of your firm's inventory, which of the following statements is true?

(A) You must disclose the commission that is charged by the brokerage firm on the confirmation statement.
(B) You must disclose the bond's rating on the confirmation statement.
(C) The sale is subject to the 5 percent policy.
(D) You must consider the total amount of the sale when determining the amount of the markup charged.

346. If an investor fails to deliver securities, within how many days after the settlement date is the brokerage firm required to repurchase the securities?

(A) 3 days
(B) 5 days
(C) 10 days
(D) 20 days

347. An investor placed a sell order on 1,000 shares of XYZ Corporation and delivered two 500-share certificates to the brokerage firm. One certificate was signed by the investor and the second was left blank (without a signature). What should the firm do with regard to the unsigned certificate?

(A) Hold the certificates and send the investor a stock power to sign and return to the brokerage firm.
(B) Deliver the two certificates as they are to the transfer agent.
(C) Return the unsigned certificate to the investor with a note to return the signed certificate within three business days.
(D) Return both certificates to the investor with a note to sign and return the certificates within three business days.

348. An investor with a credit balance in his or her brokerage account gives the RR instructions to buy a specific stock in the over-the-counter market. Which of the following orders for that issue can be executed on a single ticket by this RR?

(A) Buy shares in XYZ mutual fund for $1,600.
(B) Buy 100 shares of XYZ Corporation at a limit price of $16.00 per share or better.
(C) Buy 100 shares of XYZ Corporation at the market.
(D) All of the orders can be executed.

349. Which of the following would a registered representative be required to do if a customer passes away?

I. Sell all stocks in the account.
II. Execute all open GTC orders.
III. Cancel all open GTC orders.
IV. Wait to hear from the executor of the customer's estate.

(A) I and II
(B) III and IV
(C) II and IV
(D) I and IV

350. Most publicly owned securities are

(A) over the counter
(B) listed
(C) unregistered
(D) mid-cap securities

351. Which of the following orders are considered to be discretionary and require a power of attorney to complete?

  I. A market order that specifies only the security
 II. A limit order that specifies the price and the name of the security to buy
III. An order that specifies the number of shares to buy and the specific security to buy, but leaves the time to purchase and the purchase price up to the registered representative

(A) I, II, and III
(B) I and II
(C) I and III
(D) II and III

352. An investor wants to open a custodial account for her granddaughter, Mary. Which of the following statements are true?

  I. The account can be opened by the grandmother even though she is not a parent.
 II. The grandmother can share the custodian role with the father.
III. All the trades in the custodial account must be in a cash account.
 IV. When the granddaughter reaches majority age, the account is switched to her name.

(A) I and II
(B) II and IV
(C) I, III, and IV
(D) I, II, III, and IV

353. Customers must receive statements at least

(A) weekly
(B) monthly
(C) quarterly
(D) semiannually

354. Which of the following securities are traded only in the over-the-counter market?

(A) Preferred stocks
(B) Corporate bonds
(C) Closed-end mutual funds
(D) Open-end investment companies

355. A market maker in a stock has an average price of $15 per share in the inventory of the stock, which includes a price range of $11 to a high price of $19 per share. The current NASDAQ quote for this stock is $9.75 to $10.00. According to NASD Conduct Rules, this market maker's offering price should be based on

(A) the average cost of the market maker
(B) $11
(C) $19
(D) the current market price of the stock

356. The 5 percent markup policy applies to

(A) bonds offered in the primary market
(B) registered secondary offerings
(C) riskless securities
(D) mutual funds

357. After purchasing a specific security, an RR tells a customer that it was a good choice as the price of the security will double within a year. The RR's prediction came true as the security doubled within one year. Which of the following statements concerning this situation is true?

(A) The RR's prediction was acceptable because the security price did double within a one-year period.
(B) Such a prediction is fraudulent even if it turns out to be true.
(C) The RR should have announced his or her prediction to the general public.
(D) The prediction is permissible only if the RR had registered with the SEC.

358. What factor does NASD consider when assessing the fairness of a firm's markup?

(A) Dollar amount of the transaction
(B) Financial position of the customer
(C) Dealer's cost of the security
(D) Profitability of the dealer

359. Which of the following violate the "wash sale" rule?
   I. The customer bought XYZ calls 34 days after selling XYZ stock at a loss.
   II. The customer bought XYZ convertible bonds 30 days after selling XYZ stock at a loss.
   III. The customer bought XYZ put options 10 days after selling XYZ stock at a loss.
   IV. The customer bought XYZ call options 30 days after selling XYZ stock at a loss.

   (A) I and II
   (B) II and IV
   (C) III and IV
   (D) I and III

360. An investor wants to move a brokerage account from an old brokerage firm to a new firm. Which of the following must occur in order for this change to take place?
   I. The investor must fill out an account transfer form from the new brokerage firm.
   II. The old brokerage firm must validate the transfer form.
   III. The old brokerage firm can execute any open orders before transferring the assets to the new brokerage firm.
   IV. The old brokerage firm has three business days to validate the transfer form and four business days to transfer the account.

   (A) I, III, and IV
   (B) I, II, and III
   (C) I, II, and IV
   (D) I, II, III, and IV

361. Which of the following statements is/are false regarding discretionary accounts?
   I. A written power of attorney is required for a discretionary account.
   II. A principal in the firm must approve a discretionary account.
   III. A hypothecation agreement is required for a discretionary account.
   IV. All order tickets must be marked "discretionary."

   (A) I and IV
   (B) II and III
   (C) IV only
   (D) III only

362. Which of the following items should be on a confirmation sent out to the customer after a trade?

    I. The name of the security and the number of shares traded

    II. The date of the trade and the settlement date

    III. The amount of the commission paid if the brokerage firm acted as an agent

    IV. Whether the brokerage firm acted as a principal or an agent

    (A) I, II, and III

    (B) I, II, III, and IV

    (C) I and II

    (D) I, II, and IV

363. Which of the following statements is false regarding a broker's broker?

    (A) They deal only with public customers.

    (B) They maintain the anonymity of their customers.

    (C) They deal only with institutional clients.

    (D) They do not keep an inventory of securities.

364. In which market does the trade of securities between a pension fund and an insurance company take place without the use of the services of a broker-dealer?

    (A) First market

    (B) Second market

    (C) Third market

    (D) Fourth market

365. NASD Level III quotes provide which of the following?

    (A) Workout markets

    (B) Representative markets

    (C) Firm quotations

    (D) None of the above

366. A limit order is best described as an order

    (A) to buy at a specific price or lower

    (B) to sell at a specific price or higher

    (C) that if not executed on the day placed expires at the end of the day

    (D) to be executed at a specific price or better

367. A broker-dealer receives a bond certificate in satisfaction of a sale by another firm. The certificate has "Have a Good Day!" written across the face of the certificate. If this certificate has an authentic assignment and is accompanied by the appropriate tax stamp and a power of substitution form, then this certificate is

(A) not a good delivery

(B) a good delivery only if the writing does not cover the name of the owner

(C) a good delivery if it is validated by the registered owner

(D) a good delivery if the certificate is validated by the transfer agent

368. Which of the following would NOT be good delivery of 380 shares of stock sold from one broker to another broker?

(A) Four 90-share certificates and one 20-share certificate

(B) Three 100-share certificates and one 80-share certificate

(C) Seven 50-share certificates and one 30-share certificate

(D) Thirty-eight 10-share certificates

369. John Smith has a cash account with $150,000 and a margin account with $320,000 in equity at a brokerage firm. John and his wife have a joint account with $425,000 in securities and $175,000 in cash at the same brokerage firm. If the brokerage firm goes into bankruptcy, what is John's coverage under SIPC?

(A) $470,000

(B) $500,000

(C) $920,000

(D) $970,000

370. XYZ Corporation announces a $1 cash dividend to shareholders of record on Wednesday, February 20. When is the last date that an investor can purchase the stock and receive the dividend?

(A) February 14

(B) February 15

(C) February 17

(D) February 18

371. An investor has an account at a brokerage firm and leaves instructions to "transfer and ship," which means

(A) securities purchased must be registered in street name
(B) securities purchased must be registered in the name of the investor and then delivered to the investor
(C) all communications with the investor must be sent by registered mail
(D) all securities purchased must be shipped to another broker-dealer to be processed for this investor

372. An investor places a stop limit order to sell 100 shares of XYZ Corporation at 40.65. The tape shows the following transactions for the day after the order was placed: 40.65, 40.50, 40.30. At what price was this order executed?

(A) 40.65
(B) 40.50
(C) 40.30
(D) Not executed

373. Which of the following is true regarding pink sheets?

   I. They provide quotations and information on OTC stocks that are too small or thinly traded to be listed on NASDAQ.
  II. They provide quotes on listed stocks on the exchanges.
 III. They list the names of market makers of particular stocks.
  IV. They provide firm quotes for listed securities on NASDAQ.

(A) I and II
(B) II and IV
(C) I and III
(D) I, II, and IV

374. Which of the following orders are NOT held in a specialist's book?

   I. Stop orders
  II. Limit orders
 III. Market orders
  IV. Not-held orders

(A) I and II
(B) I and III
(C) II and IV
(D) III and IV

375. Which of the following best describes a buy-in?

    (A) The buyer of a stock does not pay for the trade by the payment date.
    (B) The seller of a stock fails to deliver the securities sold.
    (C) Both (A) and (B)
    (D) Neither (A) nor (B)

376. If there is confusion over the details of a trade between two brokerage firms, which of the following would be sent from the one broker to the contra broker?

    (A) Form 144
    (B) A rehypothecation form
    (C) A DK notice
    (D) A notice of sale

377. Which of the following changes could affect a customer's objectives that the RR should be aware of?

    I. Change in marital status
    II. Change in personal health
    III. A child who is a few years from going to college
    IV. Customer becoming more knowledgeable about investing

    (A) I and III
    (B) II and III
    (C) I, II, and III
    (D) I, II, III, and IV

378. A market maker's main function is to

    (A) sell securities out of its own inventory and charge a commission for each trade
    (B) hold securities in its own account to facilitate trading
    (C) sell NYSE securities on an agency basis
    (D) sell NASDAQ securities on an agency basis

379. A newly hired RR at a brokerage firm decides to moonlight on weekends by working for a retail company to earn more money. Who is the representative required to disclose this to?

    (A) His or her broker-dealer
    (B) His or her broker-dealer and the FINRA
    (C) His or her broker-dealer and the SEC
    (D) None of the above

380. An investor calls you for a current bid and ask price on XYZZ common stock. Which of the following quotes given to the investor from your Level 1 machine would not be acceptable?

(A) It is 30.22 to 30.42.
(B) It is currently trading at 30.22 to 30.42.
(C) It was trading at 30.22 to 30.42.
(D) It is trading at 30.22 to 30.42 subject to change.

381. Which is true of cold calling according to Rule G-39?
  I. The caller must disclose his or her name and firm's name.
  II. The caller must disclose that the call is a sales call.
  III. Calls must be made after 8:00 A.M. or before 9:00 P.M. local time of the caller.
  IV. Calls must be made after 8:00 A.M. or before 9:00 P.M. local time of the customer.

(A) I and II
(B) I, II, and IV
(C) II and III
(D) I, II, and III

382. An investor enters a stop limit order to buy 100 shares at 30 of ABC Corporation. The ticker tape following this order entry is as follows:

  29.90, 29.95, 30, 30.12, SLD 29.92, 29.90, 30.06.

The order was triggered at _____ and executed at _____.

(A) 29.95, 30
(B) 30, 30.12
(C) 30, 29.92
(D) 30, 29.90

383. Which of the following orders guarantee a specific price or better?

(A) Buy limits and sell limits
(B) Buy limits and sell stops
(C) Sell limits and buy stops
(D) Buy stops and sell stops

384. An investor purchases a corporate bond regular way and has to pay the contract price plus accrued interest up to

(A) and including the settlement date
(B) but excluding the settlement date
(C) and including the trade date
(D) but excluding the trade date

CHAPTER 9

Direct Participation Programs

385. Which of the following could claim depletion deductions?

   (A) REITs
   (B) Real estate DPPs
   (C) Oil and gas DPPs
   (D) Transportation companies

386. A friend has invested in an oil and gas DPP as a limited partner. You advise your friend that he or she can do all of the following EXCEPT

   (A) examine the DPP's books and financial statements
   (B) sue the general partners of the DPP
   (C) invest in competing oil and gas DPPs
   (D) assist in the management of the DPP

387. What is the at risk rule?

   (A) Deductions for interest expense may not exceed investment income.
   (B) It limits liability to the amount at risk.
   (C) It does not allow carry forward of disallowed interest deductions.
   (D) It limits deductions to the amount at risk.

388. When a partnership is terminated or liquidated, in what order are the assets distributed?

   (A) Secured lenders, general creditors, limited partners, general partners
   (B) General creditors, secured lenders, limited partners, general partners
   (C) General creditors, general partners, secured lenders, limited partners
   (D) Secured lenders, general partners, limited partners, general creditors

389. Which of the following is NOT an acceptable tax deduction for an oil and gas limited partnership?

(A) Depletion
(B) Depreciation
(C) Reduction of principal on a loan
(D) Interest expense on a bank loan

390. An investor is interested in investing in a direct participation program (DPP). Which of the following factors should the investor be aware of before investing?

  I. The partnership's objectives
 II. The experience of the general manager in such endeavors
III. The extended timetable toward profitability
IV. In a worst-case scenario, whether the investor has the liquidity to provide more capital to invest in the DPP if needed

(A) I and III
(B) I, II, and III
(C) I, III, and IV
(D) I, II, III, and IV

391. A limited partner of an oil and gas DPP signs a recourse loan on behalf of the partnership. If the partnership defaults on the loan, what is this limited partner's position with regard to the loan?

(A) Creditors can go after the assets of the general manager of the partnership.
(B) Creditors can go after the assets of the limited partner, who signed the recourse loan, to help repay the loan.
(C) Creditors are last in line to collect on the partnership's assets.
(D) None of the above

392. Which of the following statements is true with regard to modified accelerated depreciation on equipment as compared with straight line depreciation?

(A) It provides for equal write-offs each year over the life of the equipment.
(B) It provides for greater write-offs in the early years of equipment.
(C) It provides for a flexible depreciation schedule for the life of the equipment.
(D) It provides for greater write-offs in the later years of the equipment.

393. An investor with a tax basis of $20,000 in a limited partnership receives a year-end statement showing a cash distribution of $15,000 and a loss of $6,000. How much of the loss can this limited partner use to offset his or her ordinary income?

(A) $5,000
(B) $6,000
(C) $9,000
(D) $15,000

394. Which of the following is NOT a conflict of interest for a general partner in a limited partnership?

(A) Buying personal assets and then selling them to the limited partnership
(B) Taking out personal loans from the partnership
(C) Accepting money for agreeing not to compete with the limited partnership
(D) Acting as an agent for the partnership

395. What is a limited partner's maximum potential loss if he or she invested $15,000 in a DPP and personally signed a recourse loan for $20,000?

(A) $15,000
(B) $20,000
(C) $35,000
(D) None of the above

396. What is a limited partner's cost basis if the partner signs a recourse loan for $10,000 for the partnership and invests $14,000 in the partnership?

(A) $10,000
(B) $14,000
(C) $24,000
(D) None of the above

397. Which of the following is the most important factor in choosing a DPP?

(A) Savings
(B) Leverage
(C) Economic viability
(D) Management

398. Which of the following describes a general partner of a DPP?
   I. Has limited liability
   II. Has unlimited liability
   III. Can share in the profits
   IV. Manages the business

   (A) I, III, and IV
   (B) II, III, and IV
   (C) I and IV
   (D) II and IV

399. General and limited partners in a DPP are governed by which of the following?

   (A) Partnership papers
   (B) Agreement of limited partnership
   (C) Articles of incorporation
   (D) None of the above

400. A limited partner in a DPP steps in to manage the partnership. Which of the following would occur?

   (A) The limited partner needs to increase his or her contribution to the partnership.
   (B) The limited partner could share in the profits with the general partner(s).
   (C) The limited partner's status could end.
   (D) The limited partner would be paid as a manager.

401. A limited partnership tries to avoid recapture for which of the following reasons?

   (A) It puts the partnership in line for a tax audit.
   (B) It automatically increases the partnership's tax rate.
   (C) Recapture might trigger an add-on tax.
   (D) Recapture changes the character of capital gains into current taxable income.

402. Who is responsible for verifying that limited partners in a DPP are financially qualified and informed of the business risk of the partnership?

   (A) General partner
   (B) Registered representative
   (C) Sponsor
   (D) Limited partners

403. Which of the following information is NOT included in a subscription agreement?

(A) A statement granting power of attorney to limited partners
(B) Limited partners' statements that they have read the prospectus
(C) Limited partners can accept the risk inherent in the partnership's business
(D) Social Security numbers or tax ID numbers of the limited partners

404. Which of the following is/are benefit(s) of Section 8 low-income-housing partnerships?

(A) Low risk
(B) Reliable high levels of income flows
(C) Potential for capital gains
(D) All of the above

405. The primary considerations in evaluating the worth of a limited partnership are the

I. strengths of management
II. size of the tax deductions
III. cost of the assets
IV. amount of funding

(A) II and III
(B) I, III, and IV
(C) III and IV
(D) I and II

406. When a limited partnership is dissolved and creditors' claims are not settled, the creditors may go after which of the following to settle their claims?

(A) The profits of the partnership
(B) The limited partners' personal assets
(C) The personal assets of the general partner
(D) All of the above

407. Which of the following best describes *crossover*?

(A) When income exceeds deductions
(B) When profits paid to limited partners exceed those paid to general partners
(C) When the number of general partners exceeds the number of limited partners
(D) None of the above

408. Which of the following actions is NOT prohibited for a general partner?

    (A) Receiving compensation from another partnership

    (B) Buying and selling assets of the partnership without regard for the interests of the partnership

    (C) Competing with the business interests of the partnership

    (D) Acting in the general partner's own interest

409. Investors in an equipment-leasing DPP would generally NOT benefit from which of the following factors?

    (A) Deductions for loan interest

    (B) Income from rental payments

    (C) Cost recovery deductions

    (D) Capital appreciation of equipment

410. Which of the following rights do limited partners in a DPP have?

    I. The right to determine the income of the general partner

    II. The right to share in all the tax benefits from the project

    III. The right to inspect partnership books

    IV. The right to sue the general partner for damages

    (A) I and II

    (B) I, II, and III

    (C) II, III, and IV

    (D) III and IV

411. Which of the following statements about REITs is true?

    (A) They are traded only in the over-the-counter (OTC) market.

    (B) They are traded only on the stock exchanges.

    (C) They are bought from and sold to their sponsors at their net asset values.

    (D) They trade on both the OTC market and on the exchanges.

412. A DPP that does NOT have a legitimate purpose is known as a(n)

    (A) passive shelter

    (B) limited shelter

    (C) abusive shelter

    (D) crossover shelter

413. DPPs that invest in raw land do so for which of the following reasons?

(A) Appreciation potential
(B) Positive cash flows
(C) Certainty of income
(D) Tax benefits

Questions 414 and 415 are based on the following information:

A limited partnership has the following revenue and expenses for the tax year:

Revenue	$400,000
Operating expenses	$200,000
Interest expense	$100,000
Depreciation	$125,000

414. How much income or loss will the partnership report?

(A) $25,000 passive loss
(B) $0 of income
(C) $100,000 passive income
(D) None of the above

415. What is the cash flow of the partnership?

(A) Negative $25,000
(B) $0
(C) $100,000 passive income
(D) None of the above

416. Which statement about subscription agreements is NOT true?

(A) A registered representative must examine the subscription agreement to make sure that the information provided by the limited partner is accurate.
(B) A general partner must sign the agreement to officially accept a limited partner.
(C) The subscription agreement includes the limited partner's net worth and annual income information.
(D) The subscription agreement gives the limited partner power of attorney to conduct business on behalf of the partnership.

417. Which of the following outlines the details of the management board, powers, and limitations for condominiums?

(A) Rental agreement
(B) Loan agreement
(C) Bylaws
(D) Master deed

418. Which are sources of funding for limited partnerships?
   I. Periodic assessments on partners
   II. Installment payments
   III. Nonrecourse loans
   IV. Proceeds of the offering

(A) I and IV
(B) I, II, and IV
(C) II, III, and IV
(D) I, II, III, and IV

CHAPTER 10

Taxation Issues

419. Which of the following best describes phantom income?

    (A) Income received but not reported

    (B) Income reported but not received

    (C) Taxable income from tax credits

    (D) Nontaxable income received

420. Which of the following investments provide interest that is free from state tax in all states?

    I. Treasury notes

    II. Commonwealth of Puerto Rico bonds

    III. Revenue bonds to build roads

    IV. GNMA securities

    (A) I and II

    (B) I, II, and III

    (C) III and IV

    (D) I, II, III, and IV

421. An investor has purchased a revenue bond with a coupon of 5 percent and a yield-to-maturity of 5.8 percent. If the investor is in the 28 percent tax bracket, what is the investor's taxable equivalent yield for this bond?

    (A) 5 percent

    (B) 5.8 percent

    (C) 6.94 percent

    (D) 8.05 percent

422. Which of the following statements are NOT true regarding Roth IRAs?

    I. Contributions are made from pretax dollars.

    II. Contributions are made from after-tax dollars.

    III. Dividends and capital gains accumulate tax free.

    IV. Earnings are taxed when earned.

    (A) I and III

    (B) I and IV

    (C) II and III

    (D) II and IV

423. A Pennsylvania resident purchases a Pennsylvania higher education municipal bond. What is the tax status of the interest in Pennsylvania?

    (A) It is exempt from state taxes only.

    (B) It is exempt from local taxes only.

    (C) It is exempt from federal taxes only.

    (D) It is exempt from federal, state, and local taxes.

424. An investor bought 100 shares of ABC Corporation on February 14, 2008, and sold the stock on February 14, 2009, receiving $20 in dividends during the year. Which of the following statements are true relating to the sale of the stock?

    I. The gains on the sale of the stock are taxed as a short-term capital gain.

    II. The gains on the sale of the stock are taxed as a long-term capital gain.

    III. Dividends are taxed as ordinary income.

    IV. Dividends are taxed as passive income.

    (A) I and IV

    (B) II and III

    (C) I and III

    (D) II and IV

425. Distribution from an IRA can begin at age 59½, but must begin at age

    (A) 65

    (B) 67½

    (C) 70½

    (D) at retirement

426. What is the length of time for a tax-free rollover of assets between qualified retirement plans to occur?

(A) 30 days
(B) 60 days
(C) 90 days
(D) 120 days

427. An investor has $20,000 in long-term capital gains and $40,000 in long-term losses. How much of the capital losses are carried forward to the next year?

(A) $3,000
(B) $17,000
(C) $20,000
(D) $40,000

428. An investor sells XYZ Corporation common stock on May 1 for a loss. For the next 30 days this investor cannot buy

I. XYZ common stock
II. XYZ warrants
III. XYZ preferred stock
IV. XYZ call options

(A) I, II, and III
(B) I only
(C) I, II, III, and IV
(D) I, II, and IV

429. An investor purchases a 5 percent coupon bond with 15 years to maturity at 70. How much taxable income should this investor report?

(A) $20
(B) $30
(C) $50
(D) $70

430. An investor purchases a 7 percent corporate bond with 10 years to maturity at 115. How much income must this investor report for the year?

(A) $15
(B) $55
(C) $85
(D) $150

431. A mother purchases 100 shares of XYZ Corporation common stock at $50 per share. She gives her daughter the stock when the price is at $60 per share. What is the daughter's cost basis per share?

(A) $50

(B) $55

(C) $60

(D) None of the above

432. Which of the following is/are NOT true about estate taxes on securities?

   I. Stocks received by inheritance are always taxed as long term.

  II. Beneficiaries pay their share of estate taxes.

 III. The estate pays the taxes on securities.

 IV. Estate taxes are paid before assets are transferred to beneficiaries.

(A) I and II

(B) II only

(C) I, II, and IV

(D) II and III

433. How long must you hold your Roth IRA for your Roth IRA distribution to be qualified?

(A) Three months

(B) 1 year

(C) 5 years

(D) 10 years

434. The assets of a decedent's estate are valued at the date of death in order to determine the amount of estate tax. What is the length of time for a second evaluation to be made?

(A) Three months from the date of death

(B) Six months from the date of death

(C) One year from the date of death

(D) None of the above

435. Who is NOT eligible to open a Keogh retirement plan?

(A) A professional tennis player whose income consists of prize money earned from playing in tennis tournaments

(B) A salaried lawyer in a law firm

(C) An accountant whose income is derived from his or her practice

(D) A painter who earns an income from an employer plus money earned for painting houses on weekends

436. Which of the following taxes are progressive?
    I. Sales tax
    II. Property tax
    III. Personal income tax
    IV. Estate tax

    (A) I, II, III, and IV
    (B) I, II, and III
    (C) II and IV
    (D) III and IV

437. Which of the following statements is NOT true regarding tax-qualified retirement plans?

    (A) Contributions are made from pretax dollars.
    (B) Withdrawals are only partially taxed at the investor's tax bracket.
    (C) Contributions are deductible against the contributor's taxable income.
    (D) Qualified retirement plans can be either defined contribution or defined benefit plans.

438. Which of the following statements are true about nonqualified retirement plans?
    I. Nonqualified plans do not meet ERISA and IRS standards for favorable tax treatment.
    II. Deposits are made with after-tax dollars.
    III. Earnings in the plan are tax deferred.
    IV. Investors are taxed on their withdrawals, which include contributions and earnings in the plan.

    (A) I, II, and III
    (B) I, II, III, and IV
    (C) I and II
    (D) III and IV

439. Which of the following statements about IRA accounts are true?
   I. Deposits to IRAs are made with pretax dollars.
   II. If an individual is covered by a pension plan, that individual cannot deposit money into an IRA.
   III. The entire amount of the withdrawal from an IRA is taxed.
   IV. Deposits into IRAs are allowed up to December 31 to qualify as a deduction for that year's income taxes.

   (A) I and II
   (B) II and III
   (C) I and III
   (D) II and IV

440. Which of the following statements about Roth IRAs are true?
   I. Withdrawals from a Roth IRA are tax free.
   II. Deposits to Roth IRAs are tax free.
   III. There are threshold limits on the amount of income earned as to whether an individual can contribute to a Roth IRA.
   IV. If you have held a Roth IRA for more than five years, you can begin withdrawals at age 59 1/2 without incurring any taxable income.

   (A) I and II
   (B) III and IV
   (C) I, II, III, and IV
   (D) I, III, and IV

441. Which of the following statements about SEP-IRAs are NOT true?
   I. A SEP-IRA is designed for self-employed individuals and small business owners and their employees.
   II. Employers cannot make tax-deductible contributions to their employees' SEP-IRA accounts.
   III. Employees who are part of a SEP-IRA plan cannot make annual contributions to an IRA or Roth IRA account.
   IV. Participants can invest in their SEP-IRA accounts on a tax-deferred basis.

   (A) I and II
   (B) II and III
   (C) III and IV
   (D) I and IV

442. Which of the following statements are true about a Coverdell Education
Savings Account?
  I. It is an account that allows earnings to grow tax deferred to pay
     for qualified education expenses of a designated beneficiary.
  II. If withdrawals are made to pay qualified education expenses, the
     withdrawals are tax free.
  III. A Coverdell ESA can be opened at any bank in the United States
     or entity approved by the IRS.
  IV. Contributions can only be made until the beneficiary reaches age 30.
  (A) I and II
  (B) III and IV
  (C) I, II, and III
  (D) II, III and IV

443. The primary purpose of the Employee Retirement Income Security Act
is to
  (A) protect investors from the mismanagement of their portfolios by their
     investment advisors
  (B) protect all employees from the mishandling and misappropriation of
     their retirement funds by their employers
  (C) protect government employees from the mishandling and
     misappropriation of their retirement funds
  (D) protect against the mishandling and misappropriation of IRA
     accounts by registered representatives

444. A 62-year-old woman withdraws $25,000 from her IRA account to pay
her daughter's college tuition. Which statement is true about this action?
  (A) It would incur no penalty, but the withdrawal is subject to taxes.
  (B) It would incur a 10 percent penalty.
  (C) It would incur a 10 percent penalty and income taxes on the
     withdrawal.
  (D) It would incur capital gains tax on the withdrawal.

445. If the IRS determines that a tax shelter is abusive, what are the tax
consequences of that action?
  I. The taxpayer's deductions are disallowed.
  II. The taxpayer may be charged penalties.
  III. The taxpayer is charged interest on back taxes.
  (A) I and II
  (B) II and III
  (C) I and III
  (D) I, II, and III

446. An engineer earns $100,000 per year and has a traditional IRA plan and no other retirement plans. If this engineer makes the maximum contribution to his or her IRA plan, what are the tax consequences of this contribution?

(A) The IRA contribution is not allowed because of the engineer's income level.

(B) The IRA contribution is not tax deductible.

(C) The IRA contribution is only partially tax deductible.

(D) The IRA contribution is fully tax deductible.

447. Which of the following bonds would most likely be paid by taxes on liquor, tobacco, and gasoline?

(A) Special tax bonds

(B) Double-barreled bonds

(C) Special assessment bonds

(D) General obligation bonds

CHAPTER 11

Financial Statement Analysis

448. Monitoring advancing and declining stocks is referred to as which of the following technical analysis theories?

(A) Dow theory
(B) Breadth of the market
(C) Short interest theory
(D) Moving average

449. Which of the following are changed when a company buys equipment for cash?

(A) Total assets
(B) Total liabilities
(C) Current assets
(D) Shareholder's equity

450. Which of the following company accounts are NOT affected by the payment of a cash dividend?

I. Shareholder's equity
II. Total assets
III. Long-term liabilities
IV. Long-term investments

(A) I, III, and IV
(B) I, II, and III
(C) II, III, and IV
(D) I, II, III, and IV

451. GDP (gross domestic product) can be described as
   (A) total value of goods produced by the manufacturing sector
   (B) total value of all financial transactions in the financial sector of the United States
   (C) total value of all service transactions in the United States
   (D) total value of all goods and services produced in the United States

452. A stock is trading at $26 per share and has met price resistance at $30. A technical analyst thinks that the stock is going to break out of this range. From a technical analysis point of view, which of the following orders would be most appropriate to place?
   (A) A limit order to buy at 30
   (B) A stop order to buy at 27
   (C) A stop order to buy at 30.20
   (D) A market order

453. When a technical analyst says that a stock is consolidating, what is the analyst saying about the stock?
   (A) Going up in price
   (B) Going down in price
   (C) Forming a base price
   (D) None of the above

454. Which of the following indicators would technical analysts follow?
   I. P/E ratio
   II. Bar charts
   III. Insider trading
   IV. Odd-lot theory

   (A) I, II, and IV
   (B) II, III, and IV
   (C) I, II, and III
   (D) I, II, III, and IV

455. Which of the following are leading indicators of economic activity?
   I. New building permits
   II. Changes in business and consumer debt
   III. Sales of home appliances
   IV. Average hours worked per week in manufacturing

   (A) I, II, and IV
   (B) II, III, and IV
   (C) I and II
   (D) II and III

456. Which of the following indices is the broadest measure of the market?

(A) Dow Jones Industrial Average
(B) Standard & Poor's 500 Index
(C) Value Line Composite Index
(D) EAFE Index

457. Which of the following actions would improve the U.S. balance of payments?

(A) Americans investing in foreign stocks and bonds
(B) American companies building plants abroad
(C) U.S. banks lending to foreign companies
(D) Chinese companies investing in the United States

458. Which of the following statements about treasury stock are correct?

  I. Treasury stock does not receive dividends.
 II. Treasury stock is not included in the earnings per share calculation.
III. Treasury stock is the same as unauthorized stock.
IV. Treasury stock does not have voting rights.

(A) I, II, and IV
(B) I, II, and III
(C) II, III, and IV
(D) I, II, III, and IV

459. A company's liquidity is best determined by which of the following indicators?

  I. Quick ratio
 II. Book value
III. Times interest earned
IV. Net working capital

(A) I and II
(B) I and IV
(C) III and IV
(D) II and III

460. Which of the following transactions does NOT decrease working capital?
   I. Paying a cash dividend
   II. Declaring a cash dividend
   III. Purchasing the company's own stock using the proceeds from newly issued long-term debt
   IV. Leasing long-term equipment, which is transacted as a capital lease

   (A) I, III, and IV
   (B) II, III, and IV
   (C) I, II, and III
   (D) I, II, III, and IV

461. Which of the following is NOT a leading indicator of the economy?

   (A) Changes in inventories
   (B) Money supply
   (C) Stock market prices
   (D) Gross domestic product

462. The stocks of which of the following companies are considered to be defensive?

   (A) Oil exploration and drilling companies
   (B) Manufacturing companies
   (C) Consumer durables companies
   (D) Utility companies

Questions 463 and 464 are based on the following information:

A corporation has $6,000,000 in operating income for the year ended XX13. The corporation is in the 34 percent tax bracket and has the following items on its year-end balance sheet:

Long-Term Liabilities

6% Bonds maturing XX19	$5,000,000
8% Convertible bonds (convertible at $50 per share)	$10,000,000

Equity

5% Preferred stock ($100 par value)	$3,000,000
Common stock ($1 par value)	$3,000,000
Retained earnings	$16,000,000

463. What is the corporation's earnings per share on a primary basis?

- (A) $1.03
- (B) $1.08
- (C) $1.09
- (D) $1.20

464. What is the corporation's earnings per share on a diluted basis?

- (A) $0.96
- (B) $1.01
- (C) $1.13
- (D) $1.20

465. Low P/E ratios and companies viewed as good value, which also pay dividends, are indicative of

- (A) growth stocks
- (B) speculative stocks
- (C) value stocks
- (D) stocks of companies in decline

466. Which of the following items in the property, plant, and equipment section of the balance sheet are NOT depreciated?

- (A) Used equipment
- (B) 11-year-old building
- (C) New equipment
- (D) Land

467. In which of the following scenarios is the Federal Reserve Bank least likely to purchase securities under its open market operations?

- (A) Rising wages in the economy
- (B) Rising unemployment
- (C) Declining interest rates in the economy
- (D) Declining gross domestic product

468. When a company issues convertible bonds, which of the following are increased?
    I. Net working capital
    II. Leverage
    III. Liquidity
    IV. Potential for earnings dilution

(A) I and II
(B) II, III, and IV
(C) II and IV
(D) I, II, III, and IV

469. Which of the following ratios cannot be calculated from a company's balance sheet information only?

(A) Leverage ratios
(B) Current ratio
(C) Coverage ratio (debt service ratio)
(D) Book value

470. Which of the following does NOT have the potential to dilute earnings of a corporation?

(A) Call options
(B) Convertible preferred stock
(C) Common stock
(D) Warrants

471. A technical analyst studies the chart of a stock and describes the chart pattern as a "head and shoulders top formation." Which of the following best describes this chart pattern?

(A) Bullish
(B) Bearish
(C) Reversal of a bullish trend
(D) Reversal of a bearish trend

472. A 64-year-old investor is getting ready for retirement and wants a portfolio of investments to be steered toward generating liquidity. Which of the following investments would you NOT recommend?

(A) Mutual funds
(B) Treasury bills
(C) Good quality dividend-paying stocks
(D) Direct participation programs

473. If the Federal Reserve Bank raises the discount rate from 2 percent to 2½ percent, which of the following is/are likely to occur after this increase?

   I. Prices of existing bonds will fall.
   II. Prices of existing bonds will rise.
   III. U.S. exports will become more competitive.
   IV. U.S. imports will become more competitive.

   (A) I only
   (B) I and IV
   (C) II only
   (D) II and III

474. When a company issues new common stock, which of the following will increase?

   I. Total liabilities
   II. Total assets
   III. Quick assets
   IV. Net worth

   (A) I and II
   (B) III and IV
   (C) II, III, and IV
   (D) I, II, III, and IV

475. Which of the following tools of the Federal Reserve are used to control the money supply?

   I. Changing the reserve requirements
   II. Changing the prime rate
   III. Changing the discount rate
   IV. Engaging in open-market operations

   (A) I, II, and III
   (B) III and IV
   (C) I, III, and IV
   (D) I, II, III, and IV

476. Which investments are suitable for a defensive strategy sought by an investor beginning retirement?
 I. AAA-rated bonds
 II. High-yield bonds
 III. Call options
 IV. Blue-chip stocks

 (A) I and III
 (B) II and IV
 (C) I, II, and IV
 (D) I and IV

477. The support level is the

 (A) lower portion of the trading range of a stock
 (B) upper portion of the trading range of a stock
 (C) average trading range of the stock
 (D) moving average price of the stock

478. How would a technical analyst view a market in which the number of advancing stocks in relation to declining stocks is leveling off?

 (A) Volatile
 (B) Oversold
 (C) Overbought
 (D) Of no significance

479. A technical analyst that believes that the small investor is always wrong follows which of the following theories?

 (A) Mutual fund cash positions
 (B) Short interest theory
 (C) Dow theory
 (D) Odd-lot theory

480. What is cash flow?

 (A) Cash flow = net income + depreciation + depletion
 (B) Cash flow = net income − depreciation
 (C) Cash flow = gross income + depreciation + depletion
 (D) Cash flow = gross income − depreciation + depletion

481. A stock that moves in the opposite direction to the economy would be called

(A) cyclical
(B) blue-chip
(C) growth
(D) countercyclical

482. The economy is reaching unsustainable growth and looks like it is going to decline. An investor wants to add defensive stocks as protection to the investor's portfolio. Which stocks would you recommend?

    I. Manufacturing company stock
    II. Pharmaceutical company stock
    III. Tobacco company stock
    IV. Auto company stock

(A) I and II
(B) I, II, and IV
(C) II and III
(D) III and IV

483. An investor seeking aggressive growth would most likely buy

(A) XYZ stock with a beta coefficient of 0.69
(B) ABC stock with a beta coefficient of 1.1
(C) LMN stock with a beta coefficient of 1.75
(D) JKL stock with a P/E ratio of 5

484. The XYZ Corporation has the following income statement:

Net sales	$15,000,000
Cost of goods sold	$5,000,000
Operating expenses	$4,000,000
Interest expenses	$500,000
Taxes (50 percent)	$2,750,000
Preferred dividends	$750,000
Common dividends	$200,000
Market price of the common stock	$15
Common shares outstanding	1,000,000

What is XYZ Corporation's earnings per share?

(A) $2.75
(B) $2.00
(C) $1.80
(D) None of the above

485. *Systematic risk* can best be defined as the

    (A) risk that stock prices rise and fall in line with the market
    (B) business and financial risk of the particular security
    (C) risk of default by the issuer of the security
    (D) risk of losing purchasing power when selling the security

486. Which of the following is NOT a quick asset?

    (A) Cash
    (B) Marketable securities
    (C) Accounts receivable
    (D) Inventory

487. Which of the following is NOT part of M2 money supply?

    (A) Checking accounts
    (B) Time deposits
    (C) Jumbo CDs
    (D) Money market accounts

488. Which of the following ratios cannot be compiled only from balance sheet information?

    (A) Times interest earned ratio
    (B) Debt-to-equity ratio
    (C) Current ratio
    (D) Net working capital

489. What should you tell an investor who wants to know what a beta coefficient of 1 means for a stock?

    (A) The stock is more volatile than the market.
    (B) The volatility of the stock is equal to the volatility of the market.
    (C) The stock is less volatile than the market.
    (D) There is no correlation to the volatility of the market.

490. Which of the following ratios would a creditor to a corporation be concerned about?

    (A) High quick ratio
    (B) Low P/E ratio
    (C) High debt-to-asset ratio
    (D) High accounts receivable turnover

491. A stock split by a company affects which account on the balance sheet?

    (A) Retained earnings

    (B) Shareholder's equity

    (C) Additional paid-in capital

    (D) Par value

492. If XYZ Corporation earned $1.50 per share last year and its stock traded at $30 per share, what should the company's stock trade for if it earns $2 per share this year?

    (A) $35

    (B) $40

    (C) $50

    (D) $60

493. If a company issues a new debt issue at par, what effect will this have on its net worth?

    (A) The net worth remains unchanged.

    (B) The net worth increases.

    (C) The net worth decreases.

    (D) It is impossible to determine.

494. A company earns $5 per share and pays 10 percent in dividends. What is the dividend yield if the stock is trading at $25 per share?

    (A) 2 percent

    (B) 4 percent

    (C) 10 percent

    (D) 18 percent

495. A company has 800,000 common shares outstanding. Recently, the company bought 100,000 shares of its own stock. At the end of the year, the company has $320,000 available to distribute to common share-holders. What are the dividends paid per share?

    (A) $0.40

    (B) $0.46

    (C) $2.19

    (D) $2.50

496. A technical analyst notes that there is a major decline in short positions of a particular stock. How would this analyst view this information with regard to that stock?

(A) Bearish on the stock
(B) Bullish on the stock
(C) Neutral on the stock
(D) Indicates a signal to buy

497. Which of the following is the best indicator of inflation?

(A) GDP
(B) M1
(C) CPI
(D) Currency exchange rates

498. Which one of the following money market securities trades with accrued interest?

(A) Commercial paper
(B) Bankers' acceptances
(C) Treasury bills
(D) Negotiable certificates of deposit

499. A fundamental analyst can determine all of the following information from the balance sheet EXCEPT

(A) taxes payable
(B) inventory
(C) earnings per share
(D) retained earnings

500. Which of the following is NOT examined by a fundamental analyst?

(A) Market timing
(B) The industry
(C) Statement of changes in cash
(D) EPS

ANSWERS

Chapter 1: Common Stock and Preferred Stock

1. (D) Book value is often called net tangible asset value per share.

$$\text{Book value} = \frac{\text{assets} - \text{liabilities}}{\text{number of outstanding shares}}$$

Do not be confused by net worth, which is assets minus liabilities.

2. (D) With the cumulative voting method, each shareholder has one vote per share multiplied by the number of vacancies to be filled on the board of directors. Jason Smart has 1,000 votes (200 × 5), and he can vote the shares in any way that he chooses. Options I, II, and III are all correct, but option IV is incorrect because Jason does not have 5,000 votes. Under statutory voting, answer B would be correct.

3. (A) A right is offered to shareholders for each share owned, and shareholders are allowed to purchase the shares at a discounted price. The value of the cum-right is calculated as follows:

$$\text{Cum-right} = \frac{\text{market price of stock} - \text{discount (subscription) price of stock}}{\text{number of rights for each share} + 1}$$

$$= \frac{\$26 - \$20}{8 + 1} = \$0.67$$

4. (C) With the statutory voting method, each shareholder has one vote per share multiplied by the number of vacancies to the board, and the votes must cast in equal amounts for each vacancy. In this example, a total of 400 votes (100 × 4), with 100 votes for each director.

5. (B) In order to receive the dividend, a shareholder must purchase the stock three days before the ex-dividend date. Thursday, April 3, is the last day to purchase the stock and still qualify to receive the dividend.

6. (A) When a corporation buys back its own stock it is classified as treasury stock. Treasury stock has been authorized and issued, but these shares are deducted from the company's outstanding shares. Dividends are not paid on treasury stock, and treasury stock has no voting rights.

7. (B) The record date is the date on which the owner of the shares receives the dividend. The ex-dividend date is two days before the record date because it takes three days to settle the stock transaction.

8. (A) A limit order to sell is placed when the seller wants a price that is better than the market price. The price transacted could be at the market price or higher.

9. (D) A high debt-to-equity ratio indicates that the corporation has borrowed more money from debt-holders than the amount of capital raised from shareholders. The concept of leverage is defined as obtaining capital from debt rather than raising capital from equity. High working capital indicates that a corporation's current assets exceed its current liabilities by a large amount, which means the corporation is liquid. Similarly, a high current ratio indicates high liquidity because current assets are much greater than current liabilities. The current ratio is determined by current assets divided by current liabilities. High liquidity indicates that the corporation can easily convert its current assets into cash to pay its current liabilities. High gross margin indicates that the markup of the selling price is much greater than the cost to produce or purchase the product.

10. (D) XYZ Corporation needs to pay its cumulative preferred dividends in arrears for the two years before it can pay this year's dividends to preferred and common shareholders. The cumulative preferred dividends that XYZ owes is calculated as follows:

Preferred stock dividends in arrears

6% cumulative preferred stock × $100 par value = $6 per share per year	
$6 × 1,000,000 shares × 2 years	= $12,000,000

Current year's dividends

Cumulative preferred dividends	$6 × 1,000,000 shares =	$6,000,000
Common stock dividends	$1 × 5,000.000 shares =	$5,000,000
Total dividends		$23,000,000

11. (C) Technical analysts base their buy and sell recommendations on past price performance, movement and patterns of stock prices, charts of stock prices and their patterns, and volume statistics. Technical analysts believe that past performance of stock and the market prices are repeated into the future. Consequently, breaking through support and resistance levels indicate whether a stock (or market) is going to rise in price or break down. Based on chart patterns and trend lines, technical analysts determine how to time when to get out of the market and when to get back into the market. Earnings per share (EPS) and the price/earnings (P/E) ratio are of no consequence to the technical analyst.

12. (A) A fundamental analyst analyzes the financial position of a company (earnings and the potential for future earnings) through the balance sheet, the income statement, and the statement of changes in cash as well as the impact the industry has on the company's ability to grow its earnings. Short interest ratio is a technical indicator showing the total short sales position to the average daily exchange volume for the month on the stock or the market.

13. (C) The beta coefficient is a measure of the volatility of a stock's price in relation to the price movements of the market. The market always has a beta coefficient of 1, and so a stock with a beta coefficient of 1 is indicated to move along with the market. A stock with a beta coefficient of 1.10 indicates that the stock is likely to move 10 percent more than the market. A beta coefficient of less than 1 indicates that the stock should rise or fall less than the market's rise or fall in price.

14. (C) Return on equity is net income divided by stockholders' equity. Net income is obtained from the income statement.

15. (D) The sell stop order was triggered at $36.00 when the order then became a market order. A sell stop order is used to limit losses and is entered at or below the market price of the stock. A sell stop order (and buy limit order) is always reduced by the amount of the dividend on the ex-dividend date.

16. (A) After the order is triggered, it becomes a market order and is executed at the next price, which is $36.10 per share.

17. (A) Stop and limit orders are entered into a specialist's book. A market order is a day order that is executed at the best available price; it is not entered into the specialist's book. Not-held orders are held by floor brokers.

18. (C) With a long time horizon (at least 18 years), this investor is looking for capital growth from the investment portfolio. Stocks provide capital appreciation over long time horizons, whereas bonds provide regular income in the form of interest. In today's low interest rate environment, Treasury bonds may not provide real returns that cover potential inflation together with the payment of taxes and provide no potential growth to the portfolio. Junk bonds provide higher interest receipts but also come with higher risk of default on interest and principal. Speculative stocks are those of young companies that may or may not succeed, which could result in large losses of principal. Blue-chip stocks are the stocks of well-established companies that are the leaders in their particular industries that also pay dividends, thereby providing income and potential growth to the investment portfolio.

19. (A) The SEC provision for a shelf registration allows an issuer to register a new issue without the issuer having to sell all the shares at once. The issuer can hold back the securities for up to two years without having to reregister them.

20. (D) Trades between institutional investors who do not use the services of a broker-dealer take place in the fourth market. The third market involves exchange-listed securities trading over the counter. The second market involves the trading of unlisted securities over the counter. The first market involves trading of listed securities on the exchange floor.

21. (C) Growth stocks are stocks of companies whose revenues are growing rapidly; they have little or no earnings and generally do not pay dividends. Because of their accelerated growth prospects, investors are willing to pay higher price multiples, which accounts for their high price/earnings (P/E) ratios. Value stocks are stocks of companies that generally have low P/E ratios and are likely to pay dividends. Blue-chip companies are the leaders in their respective industries that have long established records of paying dividends. Utility companies are known for their high dividend yields due to the stability of their revenues and earnings.

22. (C) The nominal yield on a preferred stock is determined in the same way as the coupon rate on a bond issue (par value times dividend, $100 × .055).

23. (A) The investor can specify which shares are to be sold. If the investor does not choose this option, the investor is then required by the Internal Revenue Service to use the FIFO (first-in, first-out) method.

24. (C) Pink sheets provide daily wholesale quotes for over-the-counter stocks that are thinly traded or stocks of companies that are too small to be listed on NASDAQ, and include names of the market makers for the pink sheet stocks.

25. (B)

Earnings before interest and taxes (EBIT)	$4,000,000
Minus interest expense	100,000
Earnings before taxes (EBT)	$3,900,000
Taxes (40 percent)	1,560,000
Net income	$2,340,000
Minus preferred dividends	250,000
Earnings available to common shareholders	$2,090,000

$$\text{Earnings per share} = \frac{\text{earnings available to common shareholders}}{\text{number of shares outstanding}}$$

$$= \frac{\$2,090,000}{1,000,000} = \$2.09$$

$$\text{Price/earnings ratio} = \frac{\text{market price}}{\text{earnings per share}}$$

$$= \frac{\$15}{\$2.09} = 7.18$$

26. (C)
Cash flow = net income + depreciation
$$= \$2,340,000 + \$500,000 = \$2,840,000$$

$$\text{Cash flow per share} = \frac{\text{cash flow}}{\text{number of shares outstanding}}$$

$$= \frac{\$2,840,000}{1,000,000} = \$2.84$$

27. (B) Limit orders are placed to buy or sell at a specified price or better. Stop orders become market orders when the specified price is reached and then are executed at the next available price, which can be higher or lower than the specified price.

28. (A) The participating preferred shareholders receive the 6 percent dividends, but they can also share in additional dividends if the company pays its common shareholders a larger dividend than the stated amount.

29. (C) The investor paid $35,020 for 1,000 shares of XZ Corp. A stock dividend of 10 percent gives the investor an additional 100 shares, bringing the total number of shares owned to 1,100. The cost basis is divided by the total number of shares ($35,020/1,100), which is $31.84 per share.

30. (D) After a 2-for-1 stock split, the company doubles the number of shares outstanding, thereby causing the earnings per share to be cut in half ($2.50). After a 2-for-1 split, the market price is cut in half to $20 per share because there are twice as many shares outstanding. The price/earnings ratio remains at 8:

$$\text{Price/earnings ratio} = \frac{\text{market price}}{\text{earnings per share}}$$

$$= \frac{\$20}{\$2.50} = 8$$

31. (B) American depositary receipts (ADRs) are registered receipts of foreign stocks held by a custodian bank that acts as a depository, thereby assisting U.S. investors in investing in foreign stocks.

32. (C) Paying a dividend does not have an effect on working capital because the current liability (dividends payable) is reduced and the current asset account (cash) is reduced. Declaring a dividend requires a current liability account (dividends payable) to be credited to offset the debit account to retained earnings (an equity), thereby decreasing working capital.

33. (D) Technical analysts plot the advance-decline line to determine the direction of the market and indicate any changes in direction of the market.

34. (D) The quote is 6 bid and 6.15 ask. The computer quote is as follows:

Last	6.12	Open	5.85	Close	6.10
Bid	6	High	6.15	Net Change	+ .20
Ask	6.15	Low	5.85	Volume	320

35. (D) The trade at 6.15 or above the limit price could have been made by another market maker.

36. (B) The dividend yield on common stock is determined by dividends paid divided by the market price of the stock.

37. (D) When a company issues long-term bonds for cash, both total liabilities and current assets increase. Net worth and current liabilities stay the same. Net worth is determined by total assets minus total liabilities. The increase in current assets is offset by the corresponding increase in total liabilities.

38. (A) The support level is the lower level of a stock's trading range. For example, if a stock traded in a range between 10 and 15, then 10 becomes the support level. The upper level, 15, is the resistance level. When a stock breaks through the support and resistance levels, then a new trading range will take place.

39. (B)

$$\text{Earnings per share} = \frac{\text{market price of the stock}}{\text{price/earnings ratio}}$$

$$= \frac{\$60}{15} = \$4.00$$

40. (D) A reverse stock split decreases the number of shares ($1{,}000 \times 1/4$) to 250 and increases the stock price to $6.00 ($1.50 \times 4/1$).

41. (C) The only delivery that is not good is answer C. Certificates should always be in multiples of 100. Option C offers up nine 70-share certificates, which do not divide into 100 share lots, and neither does the 50-share certificate and 90-share certificate. The other three options have 100-lot multiples except for one round lot, which is broken up into 70 shares.

42. (B) The 6 percent dividend is the minimum dividend that a participating preferred shareholder receives. If the company wants to pay its common shareholders more than its stipulated rate, then participating preferred shareholders can share in the additional payments.

43. (B) Shareholders must approve a stock split or reverse split. Dividends are decided by the board of directors of the corporation and not by shareholders.

44. (D) Warrants give the holder the right to purchase common stock at a fixed price. However, holders of warrants do not receive dividends, which makes this investment unsuitable for a client seeking dividends.

Chapter 2: Bonds

45. (D) The annual interest on a bond is calculated as follows:

Interest = par value of the bond × the coupon rate
= \$1,000 × .06
= \$60 per bond

Semiannual interest = annual interest/2
= \$60/2
= \$30 per bond × 50 bonds
= \$1,500

46. (B) The yield-to-maturity of a bond is the annual discounted rate of return earned on a bond when held to maturity, and because the yield-to-maturity (4.9 percent) is greater than the coupon rate (4 percent), the investor must have purchased the bond for less than \$1,000 (par value).

47. (D) The first step is to determine the investor's cost basis in the bond:

$$\text{Annual bond accretion} = \frac{\text{face value} - \text{market price}}{\text{years to maturity}}$$

$$= \frac{\$1,000 - \$850}{10} = \$15$$

The investor held the bond for five years: total accretion = 5 × \$15 = \$75.

Cost basis is total cost + accretion: \$850 + \$75 = \$925.

The investor sold the bond for \$900 and, therefore, lost \$25 (\$900 − \$925).

48. (C) Treasury notes are issued by the U.S. Treasury with original maturities that are greater than one year. Money market securities are debt securities that have maturities of one year or less.

49. (C) On conversion the investor gets 25 shares per bond (\$1,000/\$40). The investor has five bonds so the total shares received is 125 (5 × 25). The investor sells the shares at \$38 per share × 125, which equals receipts of \$4,750. The cost of the bonds is: 5 × \$930 = \$4,650. The total capital gain = \$100.

50. (C) The taxable interest on the bond is \$45 (4.5% × \$1,000) plus the adjusted basis of the bond purchased at a discount:

$$\$45 + \frac{(\$1,000 - \$900)}{10} = \$55$$

51. (D) The only false answer is D. There is an inverse relationship between bond prices and interest rates, and interest rates would have declined in order for the bond price to go up. If interest rates increase, the bond price declines.

52. (B) The current yield is the coupon yield (nominal yield) or annual interest divided by the price of the bond, ($50/$800) = 6.25%.

53. (A) There is an inverse relationship between bond prices and interest rates. The bond traded at a discount, which means that the current yield is greater than the coupon, or nominal, yield. The yield-to-maturity is the yield an investor receives if the bond is held to maturity. The steps to determine the yield-to-maturity are:

1. Determine the discount or premium: The bonds were sold at a discount ($1,000 − $800), which is $200 per bond.

2. Determine the annual discount or premium:

$$\text{Discount/years to maturity} = \frac{\$200}{8} = \$25 \text{ per year}$$

3. Add the annual discount to the annual interest: $25 + $50 (5% × $1,000) = $75

4. Divide the annual discount + interest by the average bond price:

$$\frac{\$75}{(\$800 + \$1,000)/2} = 8.3\%$$

In decreasing order the yield-to-maturity is 8.3 percent, the current yield is 6.25 percent, and the nominal (coupon) yield is 5 percent.

54. (B) Ignore the superfluous information about the convertible bonds, which is there to confuse you. Earnings per share is earnings divided by the number of common shares outstanding:

$$\text{Earnings per share} = \frac{\$2,300,000}{2,000,000 \text{ shares}} = \$1.15$$

55. (D) Accrued interest is paid by the buyer of bonds when purchased between interest dates. For U.S. government bonds, settlement is one day and not three days. Settlement is June 6. For U.S. government bonds actual days are counted, whereas for corporate and municipal bonds, settlement is three days and each month has 30 days (360-day year).

Accrued days

March	16 days
April	30 days
May	31 days
June	6 days
	83 days

56. (C) Treasury STRIPS are issued at a deep discount and at maturity pay holders the face value of the bonds ($1,000 per security). Interest accrues and is only paid at maturity. The major disadvantage to investors is that the accrued, or phantom, interest is taxed annually by the IRS as if it were received even though interest is only paid at maturity.

57. (D) Because of the inverse relationship between bond prices and interest rates (when interest rates rise, bond prices decline), an investor in debt securities would want to invest in short-term maturities to benefit from the increasing coupon yields. The investor would not want to lock into long maturities because those bond prices will decline more than shorter term maturities.

58. (C) The quote is $102 and 4/32 per bond, which is $1,021.25. Government securities are quoted in 32nds of a point.

59. (C) Treasury bills are quoted on a discount yield basis in .01s.

60. (D) In a typical collateralized mortgage obligation, the last tranche receives the highest yields but also bears the greatest risk of not receiving early returns. Typically the first tranche has maturities of 2 years, and the next tranche has maturities of 10 years. The last tranche has 30-year maturities. All tranches receive interest, but principal payments are paid to the first tranche. Only after the first tranche has been retired are principal payments made to the second tranche holders and then finally to the third or last tranche (after the second tranche holders have been paid).

61. (C) There is only one correct statement about the purpose of FNMA and that is to provide the secondary mortgage market with liquidity by buying up selected mortgages from qualified mortgage holders.

62. (C) Zero-coupon bonds do not pay interest so there is no reinvestment rate risk or credit risk. This type of bond is subject to interest rate risk and inflation risk.

63. (B) A GNMA security pays monthly interest and returns a portion of principal to investors on a monthly basis.

64. (C) Treasury Inflation Protected Securities (TIPS) are debt securities issued by the Treasury, with interest and principal payments adjusted for changes in inflation. These TIPS offer protection against rising inflation. Therefore, declining inflation erodes value in these securities and similarly rising interest rates erode prices of existing bond securities.

65. (A) The first step is to determine the discount on a Treasury bill:

Discount = face value × rate × time (days to maturity/360)
$$= \$1,000 \times 0.01 \times 180/360 = \$5$$

Price = face value − discount
$$= \$1,000 - \$5 = \$995$$

66. (D) All debt securities do not protect against rising inflation because coupon payments are fixed. Equity securities offer better protection in low-to-moderate inflation environments because companies may be able to increase prices of their goods to consumers.

67. (D) Treasury inflation protection securities are issued by the U.S. Treasury, have no credit risk, and trade with interest. The other three debt securities do not trade with interest. Treasury bills are sold at a discount, defaulted bonds do not trade with interest, and income bonds only pay interest if the issuer earns a profit.

68. (B)

$$\text{Parity of the bond} = \frac{\text{face value of bond} \times \text{market price of common stock}}{\text{conversion price}}$$

$$= \frac{1,000 \times 55}{50} = \$1,100 \text{ or } \$110.00$$

The market price of the bond is $110.50, which is 0.50 points above parity.

69. (D) Collateralized mortgage obligations are priced and bought based on their average life and not their stated maturity. This is because many mortgages in a tranche are paid early before maturity (when homeowners sell their homes, refinance their mortgages, or pay off their mortgages before maturity).

70. (D) Subordinated debenture bondholders are paid only after secured and debenture bondholders but before equity holders (preferred and common stockholders).

71. (C) To answer the question you need to determine parity. Parity is when a convertible bond equals the price of the stock multiplied by the converted shares (conversion ratio). Parity is when the market value of the bond equals the converted value of the stock.

$$\text{Conversion ratio} = \frac{\text{face value of the bond}}{\text{conversion price}}$$

$$= \frac{\$1,000}{\$25} = 40 \text{ shares}$$

Parity price of the bond = market price of stock $\times$ conversion ratio
$$= \$27 \times 40 = \$1,080$$

The bond is currently trading at $1,060, which is less than the converted value of the stock ($1,080). Thus the stock is trading above the value of the bond (above parity).

72. (A) Income bonds are risky bonds that only make interest payments if the issuer earns enough income to pay the interest payments. Mortgage bonds, collateral trust bonds, and equipment trust bonds are secured by property, financial assets, and equipment, respectively, and are much safer types of bonds. In the event of default on interest and principal, these assets are sold to pay off the interest or principal of the bonds.

73. (C) BB is the highest bond rating for speculative bond issues. The Standard & Poor's bond ratings from the highest quality issues to those in default are:

AAA	Highest quality
AA	High quality
A	Bonds with a strong capacity to pay interest and principal but may be impaired in the future
BBB	Lower medium quality
BB	Speculative quality
B	Speculative with interest or principal payment missed
C	Speculative with no interest currently being paid
D	In default

74. (D) A refunding occurs when a corporation issues new bonds and uses the proceeds to retire an outstanding issue of bonds. Consequently, the debt-to-equity ratio remains the same. The new bonds issued are of the same face value as the bonds being retired so the corporation receives no cash. The new issue more than likely has a lower coupon rate than the issue being retired and so the interest costs are lowered.

75. (D) Money market securities (Treasury bills) have less market risk than capital securities (Treasury notes) because maturities of the latter are longer than one year. Savings bonds and CDs are not traded in a market and, therefore, have no market risk.

76. (B) Commercial paper has typical maturities of 270 days or less because companies would have to register their commercial paper with the SEC for maturities in excess of 270 days.

77. (A) Treasury bills are quoted in terms of yield to two decimal places and hence the bid yield is always higher than the ask yield.

78. (B) Interest earned on Treasury bills is not exempt from federal taxes.

79. (A) The company receives the bid price from the securities dealer of 95.04 (95 4/32), which is $951.25 per bond × 1,000 bonds = $951,250.

80. (A) A repo is the negotiated sale of securities with an agreement to buy them back at a higher price at an agreed-upon date in the future, making answer A the only choice that is not true. The difference in price negotiated represents the amount of interest in the arrangement. Being a money market instrument, maturities vary from a few days to less than one year.

81. (D) Treasury stock is created when a company buys back its own stock and, therefore, does not pay dividends on the shares. Treasury STRIPS (Separate Trading of Registered Interest and Principal of Securities) pay interest at maturity. The difference between the discounted price and the face value of a Treasury bill is the amount of interest. Treasury notes pay regular amounts of interest during the life of the note.

82. (C) The only incorrect answer is C because there is an inverse relationship between market rates of interest and bond prices. When interest rates go up, bond prices fall, and when interest rates decline, bond prices increase.

83. (D) There is an inverse relationship between bond prices and interest rates. When interest rates decline, bond prices increase. Consequently, you can rule out adjustable rate bonds, in which the coupon rate is not fixed. Similarly, an investor should stay away from callable bonds, which will be called when interest rates decline. That leaves the noncallable bonds in which the investor has locked in the nominal rate and if interest rates decline will benefit from the appreciated price in the event of sale. The put bonds give the holder the right to sell them back to the issuer should interest rates reverse direction and go up.

84. (C) Interest on Treasury bonds is exempt from state taxes.

85. (A) Term bonds require a sinking fund feature because all of the principal of the bonds is due at the same time. A sinking fund is set up to allow the issuer to deposit regular investments to the sinking fund account to accumulate enough principal to pay off the bondholders at maturity.

86. (C) Duration is defined as the average time that it takes for a bondholder to be repaid the price of the bond by the bond's total cash flows of interest and principal. Thus, for a zero-coupon bond the duration is always equal to the bond's maturity, since the entire cash flow is paid at maturity. For bonds with regular coupon payments, duration is always less than the maturity. Therefore the higher the coupon payment, the lower the duration, and the lower the duration, the higher is the coupon payment. C is the only false statement.

87. (C) The Trust Indenture Act of 1939 covers corporate bond issues. Debenture bonds are unsecured corporate bonds.

88. (A) Collateralized mortgage obligations (CMOs) generally are rated AAA by Standard & Poor's (unless otherwise stated) because the mortgage securities in the pools include GNMA, FNMA, and FHMLC securities, which are considered to be safe securities.

89. (C) Regular way settlements on government securities take place one business day after the trade date.

90. (D) The Federal Reserve Bank does not set margin requirements for government securities.

91. (A) An American depositary receipt is a receipt for a foreign equity security traded in the United States and is not a debt security. Money market securities are debt securities with maturities of one year or less. Treasury bills, repos, and CDs are money market securities.

92. (C) Series EE Bonds are sold at 50 percent of their face value.

93. (B) Repos are simultaneous agreements to buy and sell loans using U.S. securities as collateral for negotiated time periods and do not trade in the secondary market. Fed funds are mostly overnight loans from banks to other banks and do not trade in the secondary market. Bankers' acceptances and American depositary receipts do trade in the secondary market.

94. (D) The interest on the bond is $60 (6% × $1,000) plus the annual accretion of $25 ($250/10). The investor should report $85 for tax purposes on this bond per year.

95. (B) The riskiest tranche of a collateralized mortgage obligation is the Z tranche because it receives no payments until the other tranches have been repaid. A companion tranche is also risky because it absorbs the extension risk and prepayment risk associated with the planned amortization class (PAC) and targeted amortization class (TAC) tranches. The safest tranche is the PAC (planned amortization class) because the extension risk and prepayment risk are absorbed by the companion tranche. The TAC is slightly more risky because it is affected more by prepayment risk and extension risk than the PAC tranche.

Chapter 3: Municipal Bonds

96. (D) Within the list, industrial development revenue bonds are the riskiest type of bonds because they are backed only by the payments received from the corporation. Revenue bonds are next in that they are backed by the revenue from the municipal facility (toll roads, airports, hospitals, and the like). Moral obligation bonds are safer in that they have additional backing from the state government if the municipality cannot pay the debt. Public housing authority bonds are the safest as they are backed by U.S. government subsidies.

97. (A) Revenue bonds are typically used to fund airports, toll highways, and pollution control facilities. General obligation bonds are typically used to finance the building of schools because schools do not generate revenues to finance their facilities. Property taxes are generally used to pay off bonds issued to finance schools.

98. (D) Prerefunded bonds are when new bonds are issued to provide funds used in escrow to redeem a prior issue. The original issue of bonds is defeased because there are funds available to repay them.

99. (C) Interest from a municipal bond is exempt from federal taxes. So to determine the best investment, you need to convert the municipal bond to the taxable equivalent yield and then compare this yield with the other before tax yield investments.

$$\text{Taxable equivalent yield} = \frac{\text{municipal bond yield}}{100\% - \text{marginal tax rate}}$$

$$= \frac{2.75\%}{100\% - 28\%} = 3.82\%$$

100. (C) Revenue bonds are backed by revenue-producing facilities, and under a net revenue pledge, the issuer pays operation and maintenance expenses before principal and interest.

101. (B) When an investor purchases a municipal bond at a premium, the loss is amortized over the life of the bond.

$$\text{Amortization of the bond} = \frac{\text{premium price} - \text{par value}}{\text{life of the bond}}$$

$$= \frac{\$1,050 - \$1,000}{20 \text{ years}} = \$2.50 \text{ per year}$$

Adjusted basis of the bond = purchase price − amortization after 10 years
= $1,050 − ($2.50 × 10) = $1,025

Loss = adjusted basis of price paid − selling price
= $1,025 − $990 = $35 per bond

102. (B) The number of days of accrued interest on a municipal bond is calculated from the previous coupon interest date to the settlement date, but the settlement date is not included in the calculation. In regular way trades the settlement date is 3 days after the trade and interest is based on a 30-day month, with one year being 360 days, as compared with U.S. government bonds, which use 365 days per year and the exact number of days per month. Thus, the settlement date is December 12, but the buyer pays for 11 days in December:

July	30 days
Aug.	30 days
Sept.	30 days
Oct.	30 days
Nov.	30 days
Dec.	11 days
	161 days of accrued interest

103. (D) The premium on a municipal bond is amortized over the remaining life of the bond ($50/10 years, or $5 per year). After six years the adjusted basis of the bond is $1,020 ($1,050 − 30). If the bond is sold at $103 ($1,030), there is a gain of $10.

104. (D) The bond is purchased at a discount and the $50 discount is accreted over the period held. The accretion is $50/10 years, which is $5 per year. The bond was held for five years so $25 is added to the cost of the bond. The new basis is $975, which is the same as the sale price. Therefore, there is no gain or loss.

105. (B) An industrial development revenue bond is a municipal bond backed by a private company that signs a lease agreement to pay the interest and principal on the bonds. Consequently, the ratings are based on the private company's ability to service the debt. Industrial development revenue bonds are considered to be the riskiest municipal bonds.

106. (D) A double-barreled municipal bond is a revenue bond that also has the backing of the full faith and credit of the issuing municipality.

107. (C) Real estate taxes are used to pay off school district bonds.

108. (A) Municipal Securities Rulemaking Board (MSRB) rules are enforced by the SEC, NASD, FDIC, and Controller of the Currency, eliminating answers C and D. These rules allow securities dealers to give customers gifts valued at less than $100 per year. Business expenses are exempt from this rule, making answer A the correct choice.

109. (B) The only correct answer is B. The official sale notice includes the bidding details of the offering, including the amount of the good faith deposit. The allotment for each syndicate member is included in the underwriting agreement.

110. (C) The incorrect answers can be eliminated. A broker's broker neither holds inventory nor makes a market in securities. The only correct answer then is C. A municipal broker's broker specializes in trading municipal bonds with institutional customers and assists dealers in selling their unsold portions of a municipal bond issue.

111. (B) Notes are generally issued for the short-term needs of the municipality. Short-term notes (bond anticipation notes, BANs) may be issued for projects such as repairing highways, but they are replaced with more permanent bond issues.

112. (D) Municipal bonds are exempt from federal taxes and are least likely to be purchased by a qualified pension fund, which is already tax sheltered.

113. (C) Because of the guarantee from a taxing authority, double-barreled municipals are rated like general obligation bonds.

114. (B) The first step is to calculate the debt service coverage ratio, which is determined using the following formula:

$$\text{Debt service coverage ratio} = \frac{\text{net revenues}}{\text{principal} + \text{interest}}$$

$$= \frac{\$6,000,000 - \$3,000,000}{\$1,000,000 + \$500,000}$$

$$= 2 \text{ to } 1$$

A 2 to 1 ratio is considered to be adequate coverage for a municipality to pay off its debt.

115. (A) The typical order from highest priority to lowest priority is: presale, syndicate, designated, and member. The priority for filling orders received by a syndicate is generally specified in the syndicate agreement.

116. (D) Municipal bond traders do not rate the creditworthiness of municipal bonds as these are rated by the ratings agencies. Municipal bond traders do request bids and enter offers for different securities as well as position a broker-dealer's inventory.

117. (C) The Municipal Securities Rulemaking Board (MSRB) does not have the power to enforce its own rules and regulations. The SEC, NASD, FDIC, and the Controller of the Currency have the power to enforce the rules of the MSRB.

118. (A) The only form of underwriting that is not associated with municipal bond issues is the best efforts, which is mostly associated with stock issues of small companies and limited partnerships.

119. (C) Moody's ratings MIG 1, MIG 2, MIG 3, MIG 4; Standard & Poor's SP-1, SP-2, SP-3; and Fitch's F-1, F-2, F-3 ratings are used to rate municipal notes.

120. (D) Under Western account basis underwriting, each syndicate member is responsible only for its own allotment of bonds (or stocks). Consequently, Firm X is not responsible for any unsold bonds of other syndicate members. The answer would be different if the underwriting was on an Eastern account basis because syndicate members are responsible for their own allotted securities and their share of the syndicate's unsold securities. In this example, under an Eastern account basis, Firm X is responsible for 10 percent of the unsold portion of the bonds, $100,000 (10% × $1,000,000).

121. (C) The amount each syndicate member receives is based on the member's percentage participation in the account. For example, if a net order produces $5,000 in revenues from fees and each syndicate member has a 20 percent participation in the account, then each of the five members will receive $1,000 in revenues (20% × $5,000).

122. (D) The *Blue List* is a daily publication listing all municipal bond offerings by dealers. The other three publications list advertisements of new, upcoming bond issues.

123. (C) The nominal, or stated, yield is the same as the coupon yield, which is 6 percent.

124. (B) The current yield is the annual coupon (interest received from the bond) divided by the price paid. The answer is: $60/$900 = 6.67%.

125. (A) There are three steps to work out the yield-to-maturity on a bond:

1. Divide the discount of the bond by the number of years to maturity:

$$\text{Discount per year} = \frac{\$100}{10} = \$10 \text{ per year}$$

2. Add this discount per year to the coupon interest received: ($10 + $60) = $70.

3. Divide the discount + coupon interest by the average price of the bond:

$$\text{Yield-to-maturity} = \frac{\text{discount} + \text{coupon interest}}{(\text{purchase price} + \text{par price})/2}$$

$$= \frac{\$70}{(\$900 + \$1,000)/2} = \frac{70}{950} = 7.37\%$$

126. (C) Interest on bonds issued by Puerto Rico are triple tax exempt (federal, state, and local), and interest from Treasury bonds are exempt from state taxes in all 50 states. Interest from GNMA bonds is taxable at the federal and state levels. Interest from general obligation bonds is state tax exempt only in the issuer's state.

127. (A) The only correct option is IV. When selling bonds from inventory, a broker-dealer can only charge a markup on the bonds, making options I and III incorrect. Option II is also not required as the buyer can look up the ratings of the bond. Thus options I, II, and III are incorrect.

128. (A) The first action of a municipal bond syndicate in preparing a bid is to prepare the scale of offering prices. Determining profits comes later in the process.

129. (C) During an apprenticeship, a municipal bond representative may not conduct business with the public. The representative may deal with dealers and other securities professionals, but he or she may not receive commissions during an apprenticeship.

130. (A) The ad valorem tax is determined by multiplying the assessment value by the mills and then by .001: $500,000 \times 30 \times .001 = \$15,000$

131. (C) The only action that does not help to diversify a portfolio is to buy larger quantities of the same bonds held in the portfolio.

132. (D) With rising interest rates and inflation, investors want investments that are liquid such as money market securities, which have maturities of less than one year. When interest rates rise, the reduction in the market price of the bond is greater the longer the maturity of the bond.

133. (B) Special assessment bonds are not revenue bonds. They are a type of general obligation bond, which is backed by taxes assessed on the taxpayers who benefit from the project funded by the bonds. Municipalities use this type of bond to raise funds for constructing sewers, streets, and similar projects.

134. (C) A legal opinion is prepared by a bond attorney (counsel). All municipal bonds include a legal opinion, unless the municipal bond issue is stamped as *ex-legal* (an issue that does not include a legal opinion). A legal opinion is a statement that the interest received from the municipal bond meets the requirements to be exempt from federal income taxes.

135. (D) A dealer cannot guarantee against a loss of value. Insured bonds do not guarantee against loss in market value. Insured bonds are protected against default in interest and principal.

136. (B) Special tax bonds are municipal bonds that are backed by excise taxes, which are taxes on goods such as fuel, tobacco, and alcohol.

137. (A) A confirmation includes all the items mentioned in addition to other factors, such as whether the firm acted as a broker or a dealer, the information on the bond (issuer's name, maturity, interest rate, and call provision details), trade date, settlement date, bond yield, and dollar price.

138. (B) A municipality does not provide a prospectus for municipal bonds. The document that the municipality provides is the official statement. The three other statements are true.

139. (D) The rate covenant is a promise that the municipality that issues the revenue bonds will charge sufficient amounts to cover expenses and debt service fees. Consequently, the percentages below 100 percent can be ruled out, leaving 120 percent as the only viable answer.

140. (A) The municipal bond issue with the highest coupon is most likely to be called, and, in this example, it also has the lowest call price.

141. (D) By definition, the placement ratio is the percentage of new issues offered for sale this week as compared with those offered for sale the previous week.

142. (A) This is the only option that benefits a municipality: increasing assessments of property values brings in more revenue to the municipality. Rising operating expenses and increased defaults of taxes reduce revenues and are negative signals for potential investors in a municipality's general obligation bonds.

143. (D) Under Municipal Securities Rulemaking Board rules, the municipal securities principal is required to approve advertising materials prior to their use to ensure that the advertising is both true and accurate.

144. (A) The final official statement is not considered to be advertising because it is prepared by the issuer and does not require approval from the municipal securities principal. Advertising is considered to be any material that is aimed at the public and includes offering circulars, summaries of official statements, form and market letters, and research reports.

145. (D) All four are allowed to be used under Municipal Securities Rulemaking Board regulations.

146. (B) General obligation (GO) bonds are issued by local governments and are mostly backed by property taxes. Interest received on GO bonds is exempt from federal taxes and state taxes in the state of issue. These bonds are exempt from SEC registration.

147. (C) An AON is an all or none order qualifier. It is not a short-term municipal note. The other three—project notes (PNs), bond anticipation notes (BANs), and revenue anticipation notes (RANs)—are all short-term municipal notes.

148. (C) All bonds (callable and noncallable) decline in price when interest rates rise, so option I is false, which eliminates answers A and B. Option IV is false because bonds are called when interest rates decline and not increase, which makes option II true. Option III is true because in order to attract buyers to callable bonds, issuers pay higher coupon yields for callable bonds than noncallable bonds.

149. (A) An industrial development revenue bond is backed by a corporate guarantor (a private company). The private company makes its lease payments, which are used to pay the interest and the principal on the bonds to bondholders. These bonds are considered to be the riskiest type of municipal bonds.

Chapter 4: Margin Accounts and Long and Short Investments

150. (D) All three need to obtain their employer's authorization in writing before a margin account can be opened for them by a member firm.

151. (B) The debit balance in the account exceeds the equity by $10,000:

Long market value (LMV) − debit balance (DB) = equity (EQ)
$50,000   − $30,000   = $20,000

Consequently, this investor may withdraw 50 percent of the sale of long securities ($500).

152. (A) The buying power is double the value of the SMA (special memorandum account).

153. (C) With a 50 percent margin as set by Regulation T, the customer should have $10,500 (50% × $21,000), but the client's actual equity is $13,000 ($21,000 − $8,000). The excess equity is $2,500 ($13,000 − $10,500).

154. (B) The buying power is the excess equity divided by the margin, 50 percent, ($2,500/.50), or $5,000.

155. (D) The buying power in this account is $5,000 and the purchase of Chesapeake shares is $2,500. Under Regulation T, 50 percent of the investment of $2,500 is $1,250, so the investor is not required to add to this account.

156. (C) The purchase of Chevron stock at $10,000 requires $5,000 (50% × $10,000). However, the investor has excess equity of $2,500, and so the investor needs to deposit $2,500 ($5,000 − $2,500).

157. (B) The cash deposit required is $2,500. If securities in lieu of cash are deposited, the value of the securities must be $5,000 ($2,500/50%).

158. (C) Payment is due no later than the fifth business day after the trade under Regulation T.

159. (D) A client's failure to make the necessary payments in a margin account requires the brokerage firm to liquidate the positions in the account.

160. (C) A short sale always takes place in a margin account, and if securities held in a short account increase instead of decrease, then the account becomes restricted. When the short sale was made, the proceeds were $4,000. Regulation T requires the investor to put up 50 percent of $4,000, which is $2,000 in equity, leaving a credit balance of $6,000. The equation is:

Short margin account (SMA) + equity (EQ) = credit balance (CR).
$4,000   + $2,000   = $6,000

When the price increases to $45 per share, you need to determine the new equity. The short margin account (SMA) is now $4,500, the credit balance (CR) remains $6,000, and the equity becomes $1,500:

$4,500 + EQ = $6,000
         EQ = $1,500

The new SMA is multiplied by 50 percent (Regulation T) to determine how much equity should be in the account ($4,500 × 50% = $2,250). This figure, $2,250, is compared with the equity in the account $1,500. The restriction is $750 ($2,250 − $1,500).

161. (A) The investor purchased 200 shares of McDonald's stock for a total of $15,000, which is the long market value (LMV). The investor had to deposit the Regulation T amount (50 percent of $15,000) $7,500 as part of the equity portion. The formula to use is to determine the amount borrowed (DR):

LMV (long market value) − DR (amount borrowed) = EQ (equity)
$15,000   − DR   = $7,500
                                    DR   = $7,500

The next step is to determine the new EQ because the DR does not change. The new LMV is now $18,000:

LMV   − DR   = EQ
$18,000 − $7,500 = EQ
           $10,500 = EQ

The third step is to determine the margin requirement, which is the new LMV multiplied by 50 percent (Regulation T):

LMV   × 50% = margin requirement
$18,000 ×.50   = margin requirement
$9,000   = margin requirement

The last step is to determine the short margin account (SMA), which is $1,500 in excess equity:

SMA = EQ   − margin requirement
       = $10,500 − $9,000
       = $1,500

162. (C) For stock sold short with a stock price of $1, there is an NYSE/FINRA rule that states that the minimum deposit for short accounts is 50 percent of the current market value of the securities or $2,000, whichever is greater.

163. (C) The investor's equity in the margin account can be found using the following two equations:

LMV   − DR   = EQ
$50,000 − $14,000 = $36,000

SMV (short market value) + EQ = CR
$16,000   + EQ = $31,000
                            EQ = $15,000

Equity = $36,000 + $15,000
       = $51,000

164. (B) A standard margin agreement does not give registered representatives the discretionary right to trade on an account. The other three conditions are all part of a standard agreement.

165. (B) The first step is to determine the status of the account. Calculate the equity position in the account:

LMV   − DR   = EQ
$31,000 − $18,000 = $13,000

Next calculate the amount of equity that the investor should have in the account:

LMV   × 50% (Regulation T)
$31,000 × 50%   = $15,500

Thus, because the equity that the investor should have in the account is $15,500, which exceeds by $2,500 the actual equity ($13,000), the account is restricted by $2,500. The investor has no excess equity because the equity that should be in the account exceeds the actual equity by $2,500.

166. (B) The only false statement is answer B because the debit balance is the amount of money the investor borrows on the account. It does not change with fluctuations in securities values unless the investor borrows more or puts more money into the account. The credit agreement signed by the investor allows the investor to borrow money on the account and gives the conditions to service the debt and the repayment terms of the debt. The hypothecation agreement gives the broker-dealer the right to pledge a percentage of the securities in the account to use as collateral to borrow money from a financial institution. The loan consent agreement, although optional, is required by many broker-dealers; it allows the broker-dealer to lend the margined securities in the investor's account to other broker-dealers.

167. (A) The brokerage firm can pledge up to 140 percent of the investor's debit balance $50,400 ($36,000 × 140%). The $22,600 securities remaining must be segregated and identified as the investor's property.

168. (A) A brokerage firm may only lend an amount equal to the investor's debit balance when lending investor's securities to itself or to other brokers.

169. (D) An account is frozen due to nonpayment by the investor by the settlement date. For a frozen account, the investor must pay cash in advance of any purchases for a 90-day period.

170. (C) Top management who have experience in avoiding losses will implement rules and regulations that will steer the firm away from losing money on their margin accounts.

171. (C) Municipal bonds are not subject to Regulation T. Municipal bond requirements are covered by the NYSE requirement, which for both the initial and maintenance requirement is 15 percent of the market value or 7 percent of the principal amount, whichever is greater. For government bonds with maturities of 20 years or longer, the NYSE maintenance requirement is 6 percent of the market value.

$$\text{Minimum deposit} = (15\% \times \$110,000) + (6\% \times \$105,000)$$
$$= \$22,800$$

172. (C) If there are valid reasons, an extension of time for payment can be obtained from any of the registered stock exchanges or from any NASD office.

173. (A) In a cash account, if the amount due is $1,000 or less no action is needed.

174. (A) This investor does not have excess equity in his or her account. The formula for a short margin account:

$$
\begin{aligned}
\text{Credit balance} &= \text{SMV} + \text{EQ} \\
\$4,600 &= \$3,500 + \text{EQ} \\
\text{EQ} &= \$1,100
\end{aligned}
$$

The next step is to determine whether there is excess equity in the account:

$$
\begin{aligned}
\text{Equity} &= 50\% \text{ Regulation T} \times \text{SMV} \\
&= 50\% \qquad\qquad \times \$3,500 \\
&= \$1,750
\end{aligned}
$$

Thus, the investor should have $1,750 in equity in the account but only has $1,100 in equity so the account is restricted by $650 ($1,750 − $1,100).

175. (B) The first step is to determine whether this investor has any excess equity in this margin account. Use the following equation:

$$
\begin{aligned}
\text{LMV} - \text{DR} &= \text{EQ} \\
\$45,000 - \$17,000 &= \$28,000
\end{aligned}
$$

$$50\% \text{ Regulation T} \times \$45,000 = \$22,500$$

$$
\begin{aligned}
\text{Excess equity} &= \$28,000 - \$22,500 \\
&= \$5,500
\end{aligned}
$$

The investor would like to purchase $25,000 in additional stock on margin, which means that this investor would have to deposit $12,500 ($25,000 × 50% Regulation T):

$12,500 − excess equity = deposit amount
$12,500 − $5,500   = $7,000

The investor must deposit $7,000.

Chapter 5: Options

176. (B) When the options are exercised, the buyers of the stock receive the dividend. These are the holder of the call option, who has the right to buy the stock, and the writer (seller) of the put option, who has an obligation to buy the stock if the option is exercised.

177. (A) The investor has sold short 300 shares of AAPL and wants to protect his or her gains of $30 per share. To do so the investor should buy three call options.

178. (A) The last time an investor can trade an option is 4:00 P.M. EST on the third Friday of the expiration month. Options expire at 11:59 P.M. EST on the Saturday after the third Friday of the expiration month. Central Standard Time is one hour less than Eastern Standard Time so answer B is false. The last time that an investor can exercise an option is 5:30 P.M. EST on the third Friday of the expiration month.

179. (B) The firm must disclose all option recommendations it made during the past year. This list should include all those recommendations that lost money for clients. In other words, the sales statements should not have any omissions of material facts nor any untrue or misleading statements.

180. (C) This investor needs to exercise the options in order to make money because this investor is already losing money (paid more money for an option than was received). The difference in the premiums would have to widen for this investor to make money.

181. (C) The investor's cost basis is the premium added to the strike price, which is $76 per share. Exercising the call option does not create a taxable gain or loss.

182. (B) Call options are in the money when the strike price is below the current stock price, and put options are in the money when the strike price is above the current market price of the stock, which is answer B.

183. (A) The investor has a debit position because by buying a put at 6 and selling a put at 1, the investor has paid 6 and received 1, which is a debit position. If the stock price declines the investor profits, so the investor has a bearish position.

184. (D) Answers A and B are incorrect because in order to create a spread there needs to be a buy and sell option and not two sell options. If the expiration months and the strike prices are the same, it is a straddle. In this case it is not a straddle because the strike prices are different (55 and 60). Thus, the investor has a short combination.

185. (B) The Options Clearing Corporation (OCC) is the issuer and guarantor of all listed options, and the OCC decides which securities will have options. The OCC guarantees that holders of options can exercise their options.

186. (D) There are no options traded on the U.S. dollar in the United States, so answers A and C can be eliminated. The company is concerned about the Euro declining in value against the dollar, and so the company can protect its position by buying Euro puts. This action enables the company to sell Euros at a fixed price so it does not affect the company's position if the Euro declines.

187. (C) Writing a naked call involves the greatest risk because of the potential for unlimited losses. Writing a naked put defines the potential loss (the loss is no more than the stock price falling to $0 minus the premium received on the option).

188. (D) Since the investor has not returned the option agreement within the required 15 days, the brokerage firm can only enter orders to close out existing option positions.

189. (C) Stock splits and stock dividends affect the strike price on an option, the number of option contracts, and the number of shares per option contract. Cash dividends do not affect the strike price on an option contract.

190. (C) The investor bought the shares of XYZ at $45 per share and paid $4 per share for the put options. Thus, the investor's cost basis is $49 per share.

191. (C) Stock index options trade with monthly expiration intervals.

192. (B) A straddle is a put and call option, which has the same strike price and the same expiration month on the same stock. This is not a straddle because the strike price is different. The investor is long both options so this is a long combination.

193. (B) Investors write covered calls to increase income on stocks that they already own. The maximum gain for the investor is the strike price of the option minus the cost of the shares, plus the premium received from the option.

194. (D) There are two sets of calculations:

1. The investor receives $200 for selling the call and pays $400 for buying the call:

   Gain/loss = $200 − $400
   Loss   = $200

2. In exercising both options, the investor buys the stock at the strike price of $4,000, and in selling the option the investor receives $5,000.

   Gain/loss = $5,000 − $4,000
   Gain   = $1,000

The maximum gain is $1,000 minus the loss of $200, which is $800.

195. (A) The writer (seller) of the short call will profit from having received the premium, and because the stock price of the underlying stock is the same as the exercise price at expiration, the option will not be exercised.

196. (C) The investor would have to purchase the 500 shares at $30 ($15,000). If the stock price falls to $0, the investor would lose $15,000 minus the premium received ($1,500) making the maximum potential loss $13,500 ($15,000 − $1,500).

197. (C) The maximum profit on an uncovered put is the premium received, which in this case is $1,500.

198. (D) The investor received $1,500 in premiums to write the puts and in buying them to close his or her position, $75 was spent. The gain is $1,425.

199. (A) To find the gain or loss you need to determine the funds that come in and the funds that go out.

Funds out		Funds in	
Buy 100 shares	$4,000	Sell option	$300
Buy option	$400	Sell shares	$4,500
	$4,400		$4,800

The investor has a gain of $400.

200. (B) The investor purchased one call option for $500 and purchased one put option for $300, totaling an outlay of $800. Neither option was exercised, resulting in a loss of $800. For the call option to be in-the-money at expiration, the stock price would have to be above $30. For the put option to be in-the-money at expiration, the stock price would have to be below $25. Consequently, the investor lost the entire amount of the premiums paid for the options.

201. (C) Selling a put option and shorting the stock is the riskiest of the alternatives. There is no limit to the amount of the loss when a stock increases in price when the stock is shorted. Selling a naked put option limits the maximum profit to the amount of the premium, but the maximum loss is the price of the stock falling to $0 minus the premium received on the option.

202. (D) It is not advantageous to ignore time with an option. The intrinsic value of an option is made up of two parts: how much the option is in-the-money and how long the investor has to use the option. The longer the investor holds the option, the lower is the time value.

203. (C) The first step is to determine the money flows from the premiums on the two options. The investor bought the December 40 put for $400 (4 × $100). The premium is in the last row of the table in the December column. The investor writes (sells) a Dec 30 put option receiving $125. The premium received is found in the second row of the table in the December column. The money flows from the premiums are illustrated below:

Money out		Money in	
Buy 1 Dec 40 put $400		Write (sell) 1 Dec 30 put	$125

The maximum loss is $275 ($125 − $400), but the question is to determine the maximum gain. The next step is to include the exercised options:

Money out		Money in	
Buy 1 Dec 40 put	$400	Write (sell) 1 Dec 30 put	$125
Buy 100 shares at $30	$3,000	Sell 100 shares at $40	$4,000
	$3,400		$4,125

Thus, the maximum gain is $725 ($4,125 − $3,400).

204. (B) The writer of the option receives income in the form of a premium and that is taxed as a capital gain if the option is not exercised.

205. (B) Because the options are at-the-money, buyers of options will not be profitable. Buyers of options are profitable if options are in-the-money. When options are not in-the-money, sellers of options are profitable.

206. (A) Prices of bonds and preferred stocks fluctuate with changes in interest rates. When interest rates rise, prices of bonds and preferred stocks fall. Thus, an investor can protect the value of such a portfolio by purchasing interest rate calls. If interest rates rise, the value of the bonds and preferred stocks decline, but the value of the call options rise to offset the loss in the value of the portfolio.

207. (C) The most that a writer of a naked put option can lose is the strike price minus the premium received multiplied by 100 shares multiplied by five options. The most that the seller of an option can lose is when the stock price goes to $0 minus the premium received. An options contract is for 100 shares and then multiplied by five contracts. A writer of naked puts does not own the underlying stock and, at exercise, would have to buy the stock at the strike price. Thus without owning the stock (naked) the writer loses money when the stock price falls below the strike price minus the premium. The writer of a put option expects the price of the stock to rise or at best not fall.

208. (D) The investor purchased the stock at $55 per share and purchased the put option contract at $6 per share. The total outlay is $61 per share, and the investor would break even if the stock price rises to $61 per share (ignoring commissions).

209. (D) In order to create a debit call spread, you can immediately eliminate the put options. To create a debit spread, the investor has to pay more for an option purchased than he or she receives from an option sold. Thus, the investor purchases XYZ Jun 40 call option at the offer price of 3.25, paying $325; and sells the XYZ Jun 50 call option for the bid price of 1, receiving $100. The debit spread is $225 ($325 − $100).

Money out	Money in
$325	$100

210. (B) There is an inverse relationship between interest rates and bond prices. When interest rates go up, prices of existing bonds decline. Consequently, an investor wants to protect against the loss in value when bond prices decline. Such a strategy would be to buy put options and sell call options.

211. (A) The investor paid $1,100 to buy the call option and received $500 from selling the call option, resulting in a $600 debit spread. The margin requirement is the same as the debit spread.

212. (B) The debit spread is $600, so the share price would have to rise to $96 per share to break even. Using the buy side of the spread, the strike price of the call is $90 plus the spread of $6 per share equals $96.

213. (A) The maximum profit that this investor could make is $400 if the stock price trades at $100 or above. If the stock price rises above $100 per share, the holder of the 100-call option would exercise the option and the investor would have to sell the stock at $100 per share. This investor would buy the shares at $90 per share by exercising the 90-call option, resulting in a profit of $1,000. This gain would be adjusted for the debit spread of $600, resulting in a maximum gain of $400.

214. (D) The exporter wants to protect against a decline in the value of British pounds. The best way to protect against the decline in the pound is to buy puts. If the pound declines, the exporter can sell at the strike price, thereby hedging against the decline in value. Writing (selling) calls will not protect against the British pound spiking down in value.

215. (D) This investor has used an example of a straddle, which is the purchase of a call and put option with the same strike price and the same expiration. This strategy is because the investor expects price movement but does not know in which direction the stock is going to move. If the stock price goes up, the call option will be exercised, and if the stock price declines, the investor exercises the put option.

216. (C) The premium paid for the purchase of both options is $8 per share (5 + 3). The straddle positions have two breakeven points: for the call option the stock price would have to rise to $58 per share (50 + 8) and for the put option, the price could fall to $42 per share (50 − 8).

217. (D) The investor in this long straddle position could theoretically see an unlimited gain. If the price of the stock rises above the breakeven point ($58), the investor will see an unlimited profit. If the stock falls in price below the breakeven point ($42), the put option will also be profitable. Beyond both breakeven points this straddle position is profitable.

218. (C) The maximum potential loss is the total premium paid—$800.

219. (C) Capped index call options are exercised automatically when the stock price rises 30 points above the strike price (360 + 30 = 390).

220. (C) Writing an uncovered (naked) call limits the upside protection. The most the writer can receive is the strike price plus the premium received. However, if the stock price keeps going up well above the strike price, the investor will have to purchase the shares at this higher price. The other three strategies protect the investor on the downside of the price action.

221. (A) The breakeven point on a put debit spread is the strike price of the long option ($35) minus the debit spread (3). This investor breaks even at $32 per share ($35 − 3).

222. (C) The investor gains if the stock declines in price. The difference between the two option strike prices is $1,000. The net debit spread is $300 ($600 − $300). The maximum gain is $700 ($1,000 − $300).

223. (B) The investor will lose $300, which is the debit spread. Both options are out-of-the-money and will not be exercised (the stock price is above the breakeven point of $32).

224. (A) Because of the risk that all options investors face, the first step is to receive an options disclosure document (ODD) before an investor opens an account. After the investor receives the ODD, the registered options principal (ROP) must approve the account. The transaction can then be executed. Fifteen days after the ROP approves the account, the investor must sign and send in the options account agreement (OAA). These are the rules of the options exchanges that the investor agrees to abide by.

225. (B) The investor paid $6,000 to buy 100 shares and received $400 for selling the call option. The net outlay is $5,600 ($6,000 − $400). This is the maximum potential loss for this investor.

226. (B) Both actions of selling short against the box and buying put options on stock that is owned freeze the holding period. Buying call options or selling put options does not affect the holding period.

227. (C) Listed options expire on the Saturday following the third Friday of the expiration month at 11:59 P.M. EST (10:59 P.M. CST).

228. (C) The time value is the amount of time that an investor has to use the option. The intrinsic value = the stock price − the strike price, and the formula to determine the time value is:

Premium = intrinsic value + time value
7 = (35.25 − 30) + time value
7 − 5.25 = time value

Time value = 1.75, or $175 for 100 shares.

229. (A) The rule is that the adjusted cost basis for a writer of a put option that is exercised is:

Strike price − premium received
= $35 − $4
= $31

230. (D) Options are not products that are created by the company, and, therefore, their exercise will have no effect on the company's shares outstanding. Rights, warrants, and convertible bonds when exercised all increase the number of shares outstanding.

231. (B) An index option is settled in cash, so the writer of these contracts is responsible for $600 per contract ($12,500 − $13,100) and 3 contracts × $600 = $1,800 loss. Subtract this loss from the premiums received and the investor's loss is $900.

Cash needed on expiration	$1,800
Minus premiums received	$ 900
Total loss	$ 900

232. (D) Short stock and short put has the greatest dollar risk. The premium from the put gives some protection when the stock price rises to the breakeven point. Beyond that point the upward rise in the stock price gives unlimited loss to the writer.

233. (D) This is not a diagonal spread. The other three describe the spread.

234. (A) The investor's maximum gain is when the stock closes at $35 or higher.

235. (B) The breakeven point on a credit put spread is the higher strike price minus the net credit: $35 − $4 = $31.

236. (B) Before expiration of the option, the most that the investor can lose is the amount paid for the premium, $700.

237. (C) At expiration the investor paid $700 for the put option and $5,700 to buy the stock. The total outlay is $6,400. The stock price would have to be $64 for the investor to sell and break even.

238. (B) At expiration the option is out-of-the-money when the stock is trading at $67 per share. The investor can sell the stock at $67 per share minus the breakeven price of $64 a share, which leaves a gain of $3 per share ($300).

239. (A) With a 3-for-2 stock split, the number of calls is multiplied by 3/2 and the strike price is multiplied by 2/3, which results in (3/2 × 6), which is 9; and (2/3 × 60), which is 40. The answer is 9 XYZ Jun 40.

240. (B) The lower the market price of the stock drops below the strike price, the more valuable the put option becomes.

241. (C) The 30-day wash sale rule includes call options, convertible bonds, and common stock. Put options and debenture bonds are not included in the wash sale rule. The investor cannot buy back call options, common stock, and convertible bonds of the company and still deduct the loss on the sale of the common stock within 30 days of the sale.

242. (A) The two strategies that would benefit the investor from the appreciation of XYZ's stock price is to buy XYZ call options and to sell short XYZ put options. For example, if XYZ stock is trading at $60 per share and the investor purchases the XYZ Jun 60 call option for 4, the investor would profit when XYZ trades above $64 per share. Similarly, if the investor writes (sells) an XYZ Jun 60 put option for 3, the option would not be exercised if the stock rose above $60, and he or she would keep the $300 premium as a gain.

243. (B) The two strategies that would benefit an investor from the depreciation of XYZ's stock price is to buy puts and sell calls. For example, if XYZ stock is trading at $60 per share and the investor purchases an XYZ Jun 60 put option for $4 and the XYZ stock price declines below $56, the investor will make a profit. If the stock declines to $50 per share, the investor would buy the shares on the market and exercise the put option by selling at $60 per share, thereby profiting by $600 ($1,000 minus option premium of $400). The second strategy involves selling (writing) call options. If the investor sold XYZ Jun 60 calls for $7 and XYZ declines in price below $60, the option will not be exercised. Thus, the investor profits through retaining the $700 premium.

244. (C) The investor bought 200 shares XYZ at $34 per share, paying $6,800, and sold two call options for $200, receiving $400. The maximum the investor can receive from the call options is $35 per share, receiving $7,000 (2 × $3,500). Thus, the maximum profit is $600 ($7,000 + $400 − $6,800).

245. (B) The maximum possible loss for this investor is the amount paid to buy the 200 shares $6,800 (200 × $34) minus the premiums received from selling the two call options $400 (2 × $200), which is $6,400 ($6,800 − $400).

246. (A) The breakeven is the purchase price of the stock ($34) minus the premium received ($2), or $32 per share.

247. (B) The investor bought 200 shares at $34 per share and sold 200 shares at $34.50 per share, resulting in a gain of $100 on this transaction. The call option is out-of-the-money so the intrinsic value is zero. The total gain is the $100 from the sale of the stock plus the $400 premium received on the sale of the call options, which is $500.

248. (D) The writer of a call option hopes that the option is never exercised (it expires) and that the price of the underlying stock declines, which makes the exercise unlikely.

249. (D) Options do not have loan value. Long-term equity anticipation securities (LEAP) have a 25 percent loan value of the current market value of listed options with a life of more than nine months.

250. (C) Long-term equity anticipation securities have a longer time until expiration than traditional options and so the premiums would be greater than for a similar traditional option.

251. (C) An American style option can be exercised at any time during its life, whereas a European style options can only be exercised at expiration. There are no Nordic or Asian style options.

252. (A) Cash dividends do not affect listed exchange traded options.

253. (D) Only if the holder submits an exercise notice before the ex-dividend date to the Options Clearing Corporation (OCC), according to OCC rules.

254. (B) The Options Clearing Corporation does not set the premium amounts, which are determined by supply and demand, prices of the underlying stock, and other market forces.

255. (A) Index options are settled by payment of cash.

256. (D) Options on all these currencies are traded on the Philadelphia Stock Exchange including other major currencies such as the Canadian dollar and Japanese yen.

Chapter 6: Investment Companies

257. (B) The investor does not pay the public offering price (POP) of $10.85 per share because the investor is investing $20,000, which qualifies for a discounted price. This investor gets a discounted price of 6 percent. The POP is determined as follows:

$$\text{Public offering price} = \frac{\text{net asset value}}{100\% - \text{sales charge \%}}$$

$$= \frac{\$10.00}{100\% - 6\%} = \$10.64$$

To determine the number of shares the investor gets for investing $20,000, the cost per share is divided into the $20,000:

$$\text{Number of shares} = \frac{\$20,000}{\$10.64} = 1,879.70$$

258. (B) Although all four could be closed-end funds, answer B is the only one that *must* be a closed-end fund. The sales charge on answer B is greater than 8.5 percent, which makes this a closed-end fund. Open-end funds cannot have sales charges exceeding 8.5 percent and the public offering price cannot be less than the net asset value. To determine the sales charge use the following formula:

$$\text{Sales charge \%} = \frac{\text{public offering price} - \text{net asset value}}{\text{net asset value}}$$

$$= \frac{\$10.99 - \$10.00}{\$10.99} = 9.008\%$$

259. (D) All of these factors are important in considering recommendations for municipal bond funds.

260. (C) Appreciation in a mutual fund's assets impacts the net asset value of the fund. The other factors are not related to net asset values in mutual funds.

261. (B) Dollar cost averaging is investing the same amount of money into the same investment periodically. Because mutual fund prices fluctuate, investors benefit by investing the same amount in the same investment periodically. When prices go down, the investor purchases more shares, thereby lowering the average cost of the shares owned.

262. (D) Balanced funds invest in stocks and bonds in order to pursue joint objectives of achieving growth and income.

263. (B) The public offering price with a sales charge of 6 percent is determined as follows:

$$POP = \frac{NAV}{100\% - \text{sales charge }\%}$$

$$= \frac{\$10.00}{100\% - 6\%} = \$10.64$$

To determine the number of shares the investor gets for investing $50,000, the cost per share is divided into the $50,000:

$$\text{Number of shares} = \frac{\$50,000}{\$10.64} = 4,699.25$$

264. (A) Closed-end funds issue a fixed number of shares, and when those are sold, these funds do not issue any more shares. The shares are traded on the stock exchanges at net asset values or above or below net asset values. Investors in closed-end funds can sell their shares to other investors on the stock exchanges, whereas only open-end mutual fund shareholders can redeem their shares through the mutual funds.

265. (C) The first step in choosing which mutual funds to invest in is to consider the investment objectives of each fund. The investment objectives of a fund determine whether the fund seeks income, growth, or capital appreciation, which then determines the types of securities the fund invests in (bonds and the types of bonds or stocks and the types of stocks, such as blue-chip, growth, or value stocks). Once the investment objectives have been chosen, the investor can narrow the selection of funds by comparing the other factors (sales charges, 12(b)1 fees, and redemption and management fees) to make the final choice of which fund to invest in.

266. (D) The expense ratio of a fund is determined by the operating fees divided by the fund's total net assets.

267. (A) When shares are sold at their net asset values (NAVs), the funds are no-load funds, which also means that there is no sales charge. The offer price is the same as the NAV. Looking at the table, the Westcore funds have different offer prices from their NAVs, which indicate that they charge a selling fee to investors who purchase shares.

268. (A) The Vanguard Group's STAR fund is a balanced fund because in the investment objectives column it indicates that the fund invests in both stocks and bonds.

269. (C) The two Vanguard funds are no-load funds and hence do not charge a sales commission. The two Westcore funds have sales charges, and you need to determine which has the higher sales charge. To determine the sales charge, use the following formula:

Westcore GNMA fund

$$\text{Sales charge \%} = \frac{\text{POP} - \text{NAV}}{\text{NAV}}$$

$$= \frac{\$17.23 - \$16.45}{\$16.45} = 4.74\%$$

Westcore ST Govt. fund

$$\text{Sales charge \%} = \frac{\text{POP} - \text{NAV}}{\text{NAV}}$$

$$= \frac{\$16.19 - \$15.87}{\$15.87} = 2.01\%$$

The Westcore GNMA fund has the highest sales charge.

270. (A) Mutual funds and variable annuities are regulated by the Investment Company Act of 1940 so option II can be eliminated. When owners of mutual funds die, their assets are passed on to the heirs. However, this does not occur for variable annuities, which have a death benefit. Similarly, investment income and capital gains realized by the portfolio are passed on to the owners to report on their tax returns for mutual funds but not for variable annuities, where income and capital gains are tax deferred.

271. (B) All mutual fund prospectuses must include a disclaimer that past performance may not be indicative of future performance. Similarly, the prospectus must include a statement that the fund is not monitored by a government agency, meaning that the government does not guarantee or approve the securities in the prospectus. The prospectus must also include only true statements and not any lies or falsehoods. The only statement that is not true is that the prospectus can omit facts that can confuse investors. All material facts must be included whether they are confusing or not to investors.

272. (C) The public offering price (POP) of a mutual fund is the net asset value plus the sales charge. For no-load funds there is no sales charge so the POP is the same as the net asset value.

273. (D) When the investor is ready to withdraw funds from the annuity, the amount of the payments will fluctuate depending on the market value of the accumulation units. This is the most important point for the registered representative to mention even though the other factors are also important.

274. (A) The only false statement is that investors can buy shares in the no-load fund through broker-dealers. Brokers are compensated through sales commissions when they broker transactions, and because no-load funds do not charge sales charges, broker-dealers do not sell no-load shares. No-load shares are bought and sold directly through the investment company that issues the mutual fund. All the other statements are true.

275. (A) Advertisements relating to investment companies are not approved by the SEC or FINRA, so options II and III are false and can be ruled out. A principal of the brokerage firm must approve all advertising and sales literature before use. Advertisements of investment companies must be filed with FINRA within 10 days of first use.

276. (C) The annuity period is the payout period, which starts when the investor stops making annuity deposit payments to the fund and begins to receive payments from the fund. The amount of the payment received each time is determined by the fixed number of annuity units multiplied by the value of the annuity unit, which varies in value. Hence, payment amounts can vary from one payout period to the next payout period.

277. (D) The accumulation units are converted into annuity units when the payment period begins.

278. (B) The ex-dividend date for mutual funds is determined by the mutual fund sponsor.

279. (C) During the paying period, investors purchase accumulation units investing fixed dollar amounts. During the payout period, the accumulation units are changed into a fixed number of annuity units, which makes payouts that vary in amount.

280. (C) All the choices provide income, but the only fund that minimizes tax liability is the municipal bond fund where interest income is exempt from federal taxes.

281. (B) The question asks for the average cost per share, not the average price per share. The average cost per share is determined by dividing the share price into the amount invested:

For the two months with the price at \$30: $\dfrac{\$1,000}{\$30} = 33.3 \text{ shares} \times 2 = 66.6 \text{ shares}$

For the two months with the price at \$40: $\dfrac{\$1,000}{\$40} = 25 \text{ shares} \times 2 = 50 \text{ shares}$

$$\text{Average cost per share} = \frac{\text{total investment}}{\text{number of shares purchased}}$$

$$= \frac{\$4,000}{116.60} = \$34.31$$

Do not be confused with the average price per share, which is \$35 (\$30 + \$40 + \$30 + \$40)/4.

282. (A) Real estate investment trusts (REITs) pass through income to investors, whereas limited partnerships pass off income and write-offs to investors. Answer A is the only false statement. In order to avoid being taxed as a corporation, REITs must pass off at least 90 percent of their net income received to investors. At least 75 percent of the income received must come from real estate–related activities. At least 75 percent of the REIT's assets are in real estate, government securities, and/or cash.

283. (C) All the other statements are true of unit investment trusts (UITs). The only false statement is that UITs pay investment advisor fees. They do not pay investment advisors because with fixed investment trusts the portfolio of securities is bought at the inception of the trust and the securities are not actively managed. When the bonds mature, the trust terminates. With participating trusts the assets in the portfolio are shares of mutual funds, which also do not change.

284. (D) The investor receives no payments from the variable annuity during the accumulation stage. Distributions are only made when the payout period begins.

285. (C) Under the Internal Revenue Service Tax Code, a real estate investment trust must distribute 90 percent of its net income to its shareholders in order not to be taxed as a corporation.

286. (A) A bank or trust company acting as a custodian for the fund protects the fund's assets physically. If the custodian is also a transfer agent, it would also issue and redeem shares on behalf of the mutual fund.

287. (B) No-load funds can charge redemption fees when investors sell their shares, and with no-load funds, shares are issued and redeemed directly through and from the mutual fund company.

288. (A) The 1940 Investment Company Act requires that any material changes that affect shareholders' interests should be approved by a majority of the shareholders.

289. (C) Under the 1940 Investment Company Act, the minimum net worth of an investment company is $100,000.

290. (D) The redemption fee is 2 percent, which is 2% × $7.04 (the bid price) = $0.14. The shareholder receives $6.90 per share ($7.04 – $0.14).

291. (C) Shareholders who sign up for a reinvestment plan agree to all distributions being reinvested in additional shares in the fund.

292. (C) An investor has up to 90 days from the date of the original purchase to sign a letter of intent. A signed letter of intent allows an investor to receive a breakpoint, which is a discounted price on the initial purchase, even though the investor has not yet deposited enough money to get the breakpoint. The letter of intent extends for a 13-month period after the initial deposit.

293. (B) Open-end investment companies may not issue debt securities. They are allowed to issue voting stock.

294. (C) Investment companies are required to issue financial statements to their shareholders semiannually.

295. (A) The breakpoint is the dollar price at which the sales charge is reduced. An investor can use a letter of intent to take advantage of the dollar price break.

296. (C) Income from an investment company is defined as dividends received from stocks in the portfolio and interest received from bonds in the portfolio. Profits from the sale of stocks and bonds in the portfolio are capital gains.

297. (C) The only correct statement is answer C. Reinvesting capital gains and dividends increases the number of shares owned, which compounds growth in the fund.

298. (B) Open-end funds and no-load funds are bought and sold at their net asset values, which eliminates answers A, C, and D. Closed-end funds are traded on the secondary market, and the shares can be bought at a discount or at net asset value or a premium price, which makes B the correct answer.

299. (C) Net investment income includes dividends and interest and not capital gains/losses.

300. (D) The underwriter of open-end mutual fund shares is called the sponsor or distributor of the shares.

Chapter 7: Underwriting: The Securities Act of 1933

301. (C) In a Western account each underwriter is liable only for his or her portion of the issue. In Eastern accounts, the underwriter has undivided liability and is responsible for a percentage of any unsold portions of the issue.

302. (A) The syndicate manager determines the reallowance and the selling concession given to group members.

303. (B) Under a best efforts offering, the investment banker pays only for the securities that are sold and returns the unsold portion to the issuer.

304. (D) A tombstone advertisement, printed in the newspapers, is used to solicit interest in the new securities offering. It includes where prospective investors can obtain a prospectus, along with an offering price and a list of the syndicate members. A listing of the selling group is not included in the tombstone advertisement.

305. (A) The red herring contains all essential facts about the issue except the final offering price and the effective date that the issue will first be sold.

306. (D) A Regulation A offering of securities uses an abbreviated prospectus, which is an offering circular to provide information to potential investors. The other answers are all false. A Regulation A offering offers securities valued at $5,000,000 or less within a 12-month period, and Regulation A offerings are exempt from the full registration requirements of the Securities Act of 1933.

307. (A) An investment bank cannot sell securities on an agency basis, which is the role of a broker. However, investment banks can underwrite new securities, give advice to an issuer on how to raise money, and become a syndicate manager.

308. (C) Bids at the offering price or just below the offering price stabilize an offering price. Bids higher than the offering price would force the price up and, therefore, destabilize the offering price.

309. (D) All blue skies laws must be met and complied with for the sale of securities in the three states, and the issuer is responsible for registering the security with the SEC and also in each of the states in which the securities are to be sold.

310. (A) The first step in determining the additional takedown is to determine the spread and then the takedown. The spread is the public offering price minus the price paid to the issuer:

Spread = public offering price − price paid to issuer
        = $20.50 − $19.00 = $1.50

The spread includes the syndicate manager's fee and the takedown.

Takedown fee = spread − manager's fee
             = $1.50 − $0.30 = $1.20

The additional takedown is the profit made by the syndicate members on shares of stock sold by the selling group. The concession fee is subtracted from the takedown to equal the additional takedown.

Additional takedown = takedown − concession fee
                    = $1.20 − $0.45 = $0.75

311. (D) Options I and II can be ruled out because they are both factually incorrect. Stock acquired privately or as compensation must be held for two years on a fully paid basis before it can be sold under SEC Rule 144. Option II is incorrect because the SEC must be notified of a sale if the amount of shares sold is more than 500 or more than $10,000 in value. The third and fourth options are both true.

312. (C) With competitive bids for bond issues, issuers are concerned with paying the lowest net interest cost.

313. (A) The only incorrect statement is answer A. After an issuer files a registration statement with the SEC, a 20-day (not 10-day) cooling-off period begins. The other three answers are all true.

314. (B) The investor held the restricted stock for more than one year, so he or she can sell 1 percent of the outstanding shares or the average weekly trading volume for the previous four weeks, whichever is greater:

$1\% \times 2,000,000$ shares $= 20,000$ shares

$$\frac{29,000 + 22,000 + 28,000 + 24,000}{4 \text{ weeks}} = \frac{103,000}{4} = 25,750 \text{ shares}$$

315. (D) All of the statements are required for the offering to qualify as an intrastate offering under Rule 147.

316. (C) By defining the terms it is easy to see which is the correct answer. The underwriting spread is the difference between the public offering price and the price paid to the issuer. The reallowance is the amount underwriters give to the other dealers and is less than the selling concession. The selling concession is the amount the underwriter gives to dealers in the selling group.

317. (A) The underwriter can retain 75 percent of 50,000 shares, which is 37,500 shares, to sell to its own customers.

318. (C) The Securities Act of 1933 regulates new issues so option IV is not exempt from registration. Securities, which are exempt from the registration requirements of the Securities Act of 1933 are:

- securities issued by the U.S. government and federal agencies
- municipal bonds
- securities issued by banks and savings institutions
- money market securities (notes, commercial paper, and bankers' acceptances) with original maturities of 270 days or less
- securities issued by religious, educational, or nonprofit organizations

319. (B) The market-out clause is a provision that allows an underwriter to cancel a proposed public offering due to some unforeseen occurrence.

320. (A) Rule 145 allows for the sale of restricted stock acquired through a merger or acquisition.

321. (D) The selling group's determination of the stock price has no bearing on the public offering price.

322. (B) Under Rule 144, a broker-dealer is precluded from the sale of unregistered stock.

323. (C) The only untrue statement about a "best efforts" offering is answer C, which describes a firm underwriting agreement.

324. (D) Private placements are mostly issued with investment letters.

325. (C) The 200,000 shares of the affiliated person are not part of the primary offering and the proceeds of the sale of these shares go to the affiliated person. The 200,000 shares are a secondary offering. The corporation's primary offering is 400,000 shares, for which it is entitled to the proceeds.

326. (A) In a firm commitment offering, the shares are owned by the underwriter, and if the shares are not sold, the underwriter bears the loss.

327. (C) Private placements are exempt from SEC registration. Intrastate offerings in one state are exempt from SEC registration but must be registered on a state level. Interstate and variable annuities must be registered. Note that fixed annuities are exempt from SEC registration because the company guarantees the payout.

328. (B) The incorrect statement is stabilizing the issue. In order to stabilize the issue, the securities need to be sold, but they can't be sold during the cooling-off period.

329. (D) Under a shelf registration, the issuer can register a new issue without having to sell all the shares at one time. If it sells the shares within two years, it does not have to reregister the shares.

330. (B) Indications of interest are not binding on the customer or the underwriter. Investors can change their minds, and underwriters do not have to set aside shares to fill the indications of interest.

331. (C) The underwriter's agreement (syndicate agreement) states the priority in which orders are to be filled. Normally presale orders are filled first, then syndicate orders, then designated orders, and, finally, members' orders.

332. (A) The confirmation must include the customer's name, the nominal yield (coupon rate), the maturity date, and the settlement date. The current yield of the bond does not have to be included.

Chapter 8: Exchanges: The NYSE and NASD

333. (A) American depositary receipts (ADRs) are receipts for foreign securities that trade in the United States and not on foreign exchanges. Investors in ADRs are entitled to receive their dividends.

334. (C) To get the inside market you can ignore the stop orders. The next step is to select the highest bid price (26.40) and the lowest ask price (26.60).

335. (A) A specialist cannot enter orders ahead of customers and can only enter quotes between the highest bid price and the lowest ask price. The highest bid price is 26.40 and the lowest ask price is 26.60 (ignoring the stop orders). The only choice between this range is 26.45.

336. (C) The price that the brokerage firm paid for the stock is not a factor to consider. The brokerage firm/dealer must charge the market price (ask price) of $24.00 plus a markup.

337. (D) Under Rule 405, the "know your customer" rule, the registered representative is required to know the customer's name, Social Security number, and date of birth as well as the customer's investment objectives and risk tolerance.

338. (D) An investment advisor gives specific advice and is compensated in the form of a flat fee or a percentage of the assets. In order to be an investment advisor, he or she must have passed the Series 7 exam and then the investment advisor must have the Series 65 or Series 66 license. The Series 66 is a combination of the Series 65 (investment advisor) and the Series 63 (state license exam).

339. (B) With a joint account, either Mr. or Mrs. Smith can request the sale of securities in the joint account, but the check needs to be made out to both Mr. and Mrs. Smith.

340. (A) Under FINRA Rule 2790, immediate family includes a spouse, children, your parents, and your spouse's parents, in addition to anyone that you fully support. Thus, those not considered to be immediate family include grandchildren, grandparents, aunts, uncles, cousins, nephews, and nieces.

341. (B) When a market order is placed, the customer receives the best available price at the time. Mrs. Smith only receives the amount that the trade was executed for less any commissions.

342. (C) When the firm acts as a market maker, the firm can only charge a markup and not a commission.

343. (D) Under NASD Conduct Rules, a NASD firm may not distribute new issues to any of its employees.

344. (C) When opening a new account, a new account form is required. A joint account agreement is not required because this is not a joint account. It is a single account in the name of the investor, which requires a limited power of attorney in order to give the investor's brother trading authorization. A hypothecation agreement is not required because this is a cash account.

345. (D) You must consider the total amount of the sale when considering the amount of the markup charged. The other answers are incorrect. As a broker-dealer selling bonds from its own inventory, the firm can charge a markup but not a commission. The brokerage firm is not required to report the bond's ratings on a confirmation statement, as the investor can look up the ratings of the bond issue. Municipal bonds are not subject to the 5 percent policy as they are exempt securities.

346. (C) If an investor fails to deliver securities within 10 days after settlement, the broker is required to repurchase the securities.

347. (A) The brokerage firm should hold on to the certificates and send the investor a stock power to sign and return. A signed stock power is equal to the investor signing the certificate.

348. (D) All of the orders are possible in the over-the-counter market, including mutual funds.

349. (B) The registered representative would need to cancel all open orders and wait to hear from the executor of the estate. The representative should not sell all the stocks in the account, and neither should all open orders be executed.

350. (A) Most publicly traded securities are over the counter, which is much larger than the listed markets in the number of securities traded.

351. (B) If an order does not specify the specific security, the number of shares, the dollar amount, or whether it is a buy or sell order, then the registered representative needs a written power of attorney. The representative can determine the price and the timing of when to execute the order without a written power of attorney. Option III is the only option that does not need a written power of attorney.

352. (C) A custodial account is a Uniform Gift to Minors Act (UGMA) account. Option I is true—any adult can be a custodian. Option II is not true because a UGMA account has only one custodian. Option III is true because all trades must be in a cash account. Option IV is also true.

353. (C) Customers must receive statements at least quarterly. If a customer makes trades within the month, then the customer must receive a monthly statement. Mutual funds need to send out statements at least every six months.

354. (D) Preferred stock, corporate bonds, and closed-end funds are traded on both the exchanges and the over-the-counter market. Open-end investment companies are not traded on the exchanges and trade only in the over-the-counter market.

355. (D) According to NASD Conduct Rules, under the NASD markup policy the price should be based on the current market price.

356. (C) The 5 percent markup policy does not apply to securities sold under a prospectus, which rules out answers A, B, and D. The correct answer is C.

357. (B) Under the SEC Act of 1934, the predictive statement by the registered representative is fraudulent.

358. (A) Of the factors listed in the question, the dollar amount of the transaction is the correct answer in assessing the fairness of a markup. Other factors to consider in assessing the fairness of a markup include the amount and kind of service rendered, the price of the security, the kind of security (debt or equity), and the general availability of the security.

359. (B) The wash sale rule is violated when a customer sells a security at a loss and within 30 days buys the same security or anything convertible into the same security. Option I is not a violation because the customer bought call options outside of the 30-day period. Option II is a violation because the customer bought a convertible bond that is convertible into the common stock within the 30-day period of selling the stock at a loss. Option III is not a violation because a put option gives the holder the right to sell the stock (not buy the stock). Option IV is a violation because the customer bought call options (gives the right to buy the stock) within 30 days of selling the stock at a loss.

360. (C) Option III is the only false statement because once the new firm contacts the old brokerage firm, all open orders must be canceled and the account frozen. Options I, II, and IV take place in the transfer of an account.

361. (D) With a discretionary account the registered representative uses his or her judgment when entering transactions in the customer's account. Consequently, options I, II, and IV are true. Option III is false: a hypothecation agreement is required for a margin account and not a discretionary account.

362. (B) A confirmation statement must include the name of the security, how many shares were traded, the trade date, the settlement date, whether the broker acted as a principal or an agent, and the amount of the commission charged if the broker was an agent. All four of the options listed are required on the confirmation statement.

363. (A) Answers B, C, and D are all true of a broker's broker. A broker's broker maintains the anonymity of the clients and deals only with institutional customers and municipal brokers. Answer A is false; they do not deal with public customers.

364. (D) Trades between institutions without the use of a broker-dealer takes place in the fourth market through the use of electronic communications networks (ECNs).

365. (C) All NASD Level III quotes are firm in that the dealer must buy and sell a minimum of 100 shares at the prices quoted.

366. (D) Answer A describes only the buy side of a limit order, and answer B describes only the sell side of a limit order. Limit orders do not expire at the end of the day if not executed. Market orders expire at the end of the day if they are not executed.

367. (D) Because the certificate has writing on its face and is mutilated, it must be validated by either the issuer of the bond or its authorized agent, which includes the transfer agent in order for it to be a good delivery.

368. (A) The delivery of four 90-share certificates and one 20-share certificate cannot be combined into 100-share lots and is, therefore, bad delivery.

369. (C) John can get up to $500,000 in each account, which includes no more than $100,000 in cash for each account. He would be covered for $320,000 in his margin account and $100,000 in his cash account, for a total of $420,000. In his joint account, which is treated as a separate customer, he would receive $400,000 in securities and $100,000 in cash. His total coverage is $920,000 ($420,000 + $500,000).

370. (B) The record date is two days after the ex-dividend date, February 18. The investor needs to buy the stock the day before the ex-dividend date to get the dividend. February 17 is a Sunday and so Friday, February 15, is the last day to purchase the stock and receive the dividend.

371. (B) *To transfer and ship* means that the investor wants the securities purchased to be registered in the investor's name (and not in street name) and then delivered to the investor.

372. (D) A stop limit order at 40.65 is triggered at 40.65, but then the price never gets back to the limit price of 40.65, so the order is not executed for that day.

373. (C) Options I and III are true. Pink sheets do not provide information on exchange-listed stocks or NASDAQ stocks so options II and IV are false.

374. (D) The specialist keeps track of limit and stop orders in the book. Market orders are executed after being placed at the best available price and, therefore, are not entered in a specialist's book. Not-held orders are held by floor brokers who use their discretion regarding the time and price that the orders are filled.

375. (B) A buy-in occurs when the seller does not deliver the securities sold. The brokerage firm would then need to buy the securities from another investor in order to deliver them to the purchaser. The seller's account (the seller who failed to deliver the securities) is frozen for 90 days, necessitating that any purchases be paid for in advance and any securities sold be delivered before they can be sold.

376. (C) When there is confusion over the details of a trade, one of the brokerage firms sends the other firm a don't know (DK) notice, which is used for unmatched or uncompared trades. A Form 144 is filed with the SEC when insiders sell stock or when stock issued through a private placement is sold. Rehypothecation forms are used for margin accounts.

377. (D) The registered representative should be aware of all the choices listed because they can change the customer's investment objectives. A change in marital status often changes investment objectives as the customer may become more conservative in the choice of investments. Similarly, a change in health status might necessitate a different asset allocation plan. To support a child going to college requires investments that will fund those costs. A more knowledgeable investor might want to steer his or her investments in a different direction from the representative's plan.

378. (B) Answer A can be ruled out because a market maker charges a markup or markdown and not a commission. Answers C and D are also incorrect because market makers act as principals in trades and not as agents. Market makers do sell securities out of their own inventory to facilitate trading.

379. (A) Moonlighting rules require registered representatives to disclose this information to their employers (broker-dealers).

380. (A) The only quote that is unacceptable is answer A, because it states a definite price that the investor can buy or sell at. This is unacceptable unless your brokerage firm is also a market maker in the stock and you can guarantee that price. The other three quotes are acceptable because the prices are all subject to change.

381. (B) Rule G-39 covers cold-calling potential customers. The registered representative must make calls between 8:00 A.M. and 9:00 P.M. local time of the potential customer. The registered representative must disclose his or her name, the brokerage firm's name, and the firm's telephone number and/or address along with the fact that the call is a sales call.

382. (D) There are two parts to this order. The first is a buy stop order at 30, which means that the order is triggered when the price of the stock reaches 30. The second part of the order is to buy the stock at 30 or below. The order is not executed at 29.92 because SLD means that the trade was reported out of sequence and you need to go to the next trade at 30 or below. The next trade is 29.90, which is the executed price.

383. (A) Orders that are transacted at a specified price or better are limit orders. For example, a limit order to buy at $30 is executed only if the stock falls to $30 per share or below. A $30 sell limit order is executed only if the stock rises to $30 or more. Stop orders to buy or sell are only triggered after the specified stop prices are reached, and then turn into market orders. The executed price could be above, at, or below the specified price.

384. (B) For bonds, accrued interest is always paid up to but not including the settlement date. For corporate bonds, each month is figured to have 30 days, irrespective of the number of days in the month. Interest accrual includes the coupon date.

Chapter 9: Direct Participation Programs

385. (C) Oil and gas along with mining companies that mine natural resources can claim depletion deductions. Depletion, like depreciation, is a tax deduction for mining the decreasing supply of natural resources from the earth.

386. (D) A limited partner in a direct participation program cannot assist in managing the partnership. Limited partners can examine the books of the partnership, sue the general partners, and invest in competing oil and gas partnerships.

387. (D) The at risk rule is important in that it limits deductions to the amount contributed (at risk).

388. (A) In termination or liquidation of a partnership, secured lenders are paid first, followed by general creditors, limited partners, and then general partners.

389. (C) The prepayment of principal on a loan is not a deductible expense. The other options (depletion, depreciation, and interest expense) are acceptable tax deductions.

390. (D) The investor should be aware of all four factors. The direct participation program's objectives are important. The general manager's experience shows whether this manager has been successful in the past. The timetable indicates how long the investor is expected to wait until the project becomes profitable. If the partnership project runs into problems, the investor might have to put in more money and would need the liquidity to be able to do so.

391. (B) In the case of a default, the limited partner, who signed the recourse loan, allow creditors to go after that limited partner's assets to help in repaying the loan.

392. (B) Modified accelerated depreciation allows a company to write off a higher percentage in depreciation in the early years of the life of the equipment than the level amounts in straight line depreciation. Near the end of the life of the equipment, the accelerated depreciation amounts are less than the level amounts in straight line depreciation.

393. (A) The cash distribution of $15,000 received by the limited partner reduces the tax basis to $5,000 ($20,000 − $15,000). For limited partners, the loss deducted against ordinary income cannot exceed the tax basis. Therefore, only $5,000 of the $6,000 loss can be deducted in that year.

394. (D) Answers A, B, and C are all actions that are conflicts of interest for the general partner in a limited partnership. It is not a conflict of interest for a general manager to act as an agent on behalf of the limited partnership.

395. (C) The limited partner is liable for the $20,000 recourse loan and the potential loss of his or her $15,000 investment. Therefore, the maximum potential loss is $35,000.

396. (C) The investment of $14,000 plus the $10,000 for the recourse loan are part of the partner's cost basis, for a total of $24,000.

397. (C) Economic viability is the most important factor in choosing a direct participation program (DPP). If the DPP is not economically viable, the management and the other factors are of no significance.

398. (B) The only characteristic that does not apply to a general partner is option I, limited liability. A general partner has unlimited liability in a partnership, can share in the profits, and can manage the business.

399. (B) Agreement of limited partnership contains the rules, rights, limitations, and obligations of the general and limited partners.

400. (C) If a limited partner participates in the management of the partnership, then the limited partner's status as a limited partner is jeopardized.

401. (D) Recapture turns capital gains into current taxable income. The other three answers are false because partnerships do not pay taxes (the partners pay their share of the profits).

402. (B) The registered representative is responsible for verifying that limited partners meet the net worth and income requirements and are informed of the nature of the business and the risks of the partnership.

403. (A) The subscription agreement does not contain statements granting limited partners the power of attorney. The general partner is granted power of attorney. The subscription agreement contains the limited partners' names, addresses, and Social Security numbers along with partners' statements that each partner is qualified as to income and net worth, has read the prospectus, and can accept the risk inherent in the business of the partnership.

404. (A) These projects are low risk due mainly to guarantees from the government.

405. (B) The size of the tax deduction is not as important in determining the worth of a limited partnership. The strength of management (competency of the general manager), the cost of the assets, and the adequacy of funding are more important in determining the worth of the partnership.

406. (C) When claims are not settled by the dissolution of the partnership, creditors can go after the personal assets of the general partner to settle their claims.

407. (A) Crossover is when income exceeds deductions in the limited partnership.

408. (A) The general partner may also be a general partner in another limited partnership and is entitled to receive compensation from both partnerships.

409. (D) An equipment-leasing direct participation program usually has equipment that declines in value as it is depreciated over its useful life and, therefore, would not result in any appreciation.

410. (D) Limited partners have the right to inspect the partnership's books and the right to sue the general partner for damages. A limited partner does not have the right to determine the income of the general partner, which is determined in the original agreement. Limited partners do not have the right to share in all the tax benefits of the partnership. They would need to share these benefits with the general partner.

411. (D) Real estate investment trusts trade on both the over-the-counter market and the stock exchanges similar to closed-end funds.

412. (C) Direct participation programs that are set up primarily for tax purposes to create tax deductions, without a legitimate business purpose, are known as abusive shelters and can be opposed by the Internal Revenue Service.

413. (A) Investing in raw land is speculative and generally done for the potential appreciation. Raw land offers no income or tax benefits, and after paying property taxes has negative cash flows.

414. (A) The limited partnership reports a $25,000 passive loss to its partners. Unless the partners have passive income to offset against the loss, there will not be any taxable consequences.

415. (C) There is positive cash flow of $100,000 (depreciation of $125,000 − $25,000 loss).

416. (D) Limited partners cannot make decisions for the partnership. All the other answers are true.

417. (C) The bylaws of a condominium detail the powers and restrictions and responsibilities of management.

418. (D) All of the statements include sources of funding for limited partnerships.

Chapter 10: Taxation Issues

419. (B) Phantom income is income that is reported even though it has not been received. An example is a zero-coupon bond, which does not pay interest but each year interest is imputed and reported to the owner even though the interest is not received. The zero-coupon bondholder pays taxes on the imputed interest creating a negative cash flow.

420. (A) Interest received from Treasury notes is tax deductible at the state level (in all states), as is interest from bonds issued by the Commonwealth of Puerto Rico. In addition, interest from bonds issued by the Commonwealth of Puerto Rico is also exempt from federal and local taxes. Interest on revenue bonds is only exempt in the state in which the bonds were issued. Interest on GNMA securities is taxable at the federal, state, and local levels.

421. (D)

The taxable equivalent yield $= \dfrac{\text{tax-free yield}}{(1 - \text{marginal tax rate})}$

$$= \dfrac{0.058}{(1 - 0.28)} = 8.055\%$$

422. (B) Contributions to a Roth IRA are made from after-tax dollars, and dividends and capital gains accumulate tax free.

423. (D) Interest on a Pennsylvania municipal bond is exempt from federal, state, and local taxes for Pennsylvania residents. Similarly, interest received on U.S. territory bonds (Guam; Samoa; Washington, D.C.; Puerto Rico; and U.S. Virgin Islands) is also triple tax exempt.

424. (C) The holding period for capital gains to be considered long tem is longer than one year. This investor held the stock for exactly one year, which makes the gain short term. Dividends are taxed as ordinary income. Limited partnerships are the source of passive income.

425. (C) With an IRA, age 70½ is the age at which withdrawals must begin.

426. (B) For the rollover to be tax free, the transfer must occur within 60 days.

427. (B) The investor has a net long-term capital loss of $20,000 ($40,000 − $20,000). The investor can deduct $3,000 of that capital loss against earned income and the additional loss of $17,000 is carried forward to the next year to be offset against capital gains incurred.

428. (D) Because the investor sold the common stock at a loss, this investor cannot buy back the same security or any security that is convertible into common stock of the company within 30 days to avoid the wash sale rule. Preferred stock is a different security, which is not convertible into common stock (unless it is convertible preferred stock). Thus, this investor can purchase XYZ preferred stock within 30 days. The investor cannot buy call options or warrants that may be exercised to give the investor the right to buy the common stock at a fixed price. To summarize, the investor can buy put options on XYZ (the right to sell), XYZ bonds, and XYZ preferred stock within 30 days.

429. (D) The investor purchased the bond at a discount $70 ($700). The bond matures at par $1,000, and this $300 difference must be adjusted over the life of the bond:

$$\frac{\$300}{15 \text{ yrs}} = \$20 \text{ per year}$$

This $20 accretion per year is added to the coupon interest received ($20 + $50) to report $70 of taxable income.

430. (B) The investor paid a premium price for the bond, $1,150. Since the bond matures at par, $1,000, the $150 premium must be amortized over the life of the bond ($150/10 = $15 per year). The amount of income reported for each year is $55 ($70 − $15). Corporate bondholders have the option of whether or not to amortize their premium bonds.

431. (A) The daughter assumes the cost basis of $50 per share, which is the purchase price. When common stock is given as a gift, the cost basis is the donor's purchase price if the stock has appreciated in value. If the stock has gone down below the donor's purchase price when the donor gifts the stock, the cost basis of the stock is valued on the date of the gift.

432. (B) The only incorrect statement is option II. Beneficiaries do not pay the tax liabilities of the estate. The estate pays the taxes on securities before they are transferred to beneficiaries. Inherited stocks are always taxed as long term.

433. (C) You must hold your Roth IRA for at least five years in order for your Roth IRA distribution to be qualified.

434. (B) The second evaluation is made six months from the date of death. The estate has a choice of using either the date of death or six months from the date of death to value the estate.

435. (B) A Keogh account can be opened by people with self-employed income. People who are salaried are ineligible for opening Keogh accounts. A salaried individual who earns monies from supplemental self-employment activities can open a Keogh retirement account.

436. (D) Progressive taxes include personal income tax, estate tax, and gift tax. For taxes to be progressive, the more taxable money an individual has the higher the tax rate. A regressive tax affects lower income individuals more than higher income individuals. For example, a sales tax of 6 percent affects low income taxpayers more than higher income taxpayers. Some regressive taxes are sales, property, payroll, excise, and gasoline taxes.

437. (B) The only incorrect statement about qualified retirement plans is answer B. Because contributions are deductible against your taxable income and the contributions are made with pretax dollars, the entire withdrawal is taxed at the investor's tax bracket. The entire amount includes the contributions and the earnings on the contributions.

438. (A) The only untrue statement is choice IV. Withdrawals from a nonqualified retirement plan are taxed only on the amount above contributions made. The other three statements are true about nonqualified retirement plans.

439. (C) Deposits to IRAs are tax deductible so they are made with pretax dollars. Because contributions are tax deductible, the entire amount of the withdrawals is taxed. The entire amount includes contributions and earnings. The incorrect statements are choices II and IV. An individual covered by a pension plan can deposit money into an IRA account. Whether the contributions are tax deductible or not depends on the amount the individual earns. Deposits into IRAs are allowed up to April 15, to qualify as a deduction for the previous year's income taxes.

440. (D) Option II is incorrect. Because contributions are not tax deductible, the entire withdrawal is not taxed, provided that the Roth IRA account has been held for five years and the owner of the account has attained age 59½.

441. (B) The two false statements about SEP-IRA accounts are options II and III. Employers can make tax-deductible contributions to the accounts of their employees. Employees can make annual contributions to IRA or Roth IRA accounts.

442. (C) The only incorrect statement about Coverdell ESAs is that the beneficiary must be under age 30. A beneficiary must be under the age of 18 years or a special needs beneficiary.

443. (B) The Employee Retirement Income Security Act's primary purpose is to protect employees from the mishandling and misappropriation of their pension plan assets by unions and corporations.

444. (A) Withdrawals from an IRA before reaching age 59½ would incur a 10 percent penalty. After age 59½, withdrawals do not incur a 10 percent penalty but withdrawals are subject to income taxes.

445. (D) If the IRS deems a tax shelter abusive, it can disallow deductions made to the shelter and can charge back interest and penalties.

446. (D) If the engineer is not covered by any other retirement plan, the engineer can make the maximum contribution to the traditional IRA plan. The contribution is tax deductible.

447. (A) Interest and principal on special tax bonds are paid from special taxes on tobacco, liquor, and gasoline.

Chapter 11: Financial Statement Analysis

448. (B) Using advancing and declining stocks is an attempt to predict the future direction of the market. This theory is referred to as the breadth of the market.

449. (C) When equipment is purchased for cash, the cash account is reduced, which affects current assets. Total assets are not affected because cash is reduced but equipment is increased by the same amount as the reduction in cash. Total liabilities and shareholder's equity are not affected.

450. (A) Payment of a cash dividend affects the cash account, which reduces current assets and affects current liabilities. Long-term liabilities, long-term investments, and shareholder's equity are not affected by this transaction.

451. (D) This answer provides the definition of GDP.

452. (C) A technical analyst would only want to buy the stock if it breaks out in price above $30 per share. A stop order to buy at $30.20 would only be executed if the stock reaches $30.20.

453. (C) Forming a base price means that the stock price is not moving much in either direction, which is the same as consolidating.

454. (B) A technical analyst is only concerned with price movements, volume, and trends. These indicators include bar charts (all forms of charting price movements), insider trading, and odd-lot trading. Fundamental analysts are concerned with finding stocks below their intrinsic value and would be concerned with financial statement analysis such as using P/E ratios in their quest for undervalued stocks.

455. (A) The only lagging indicator is the sale of home appliances. The other three indicators are leading indicators of economic activity.

456. (C) The Value Line Composite Index uses 1,700 stocks listed on the NYSE, AMEX, and OTC markets and, therefore, is the broadest measure of the market. The EAFE Index is a benchmark for foreign stocks and foreign stock mutual funds, which includes 1,026 stocks from 20 countries. The Standard & Poor's 500 Index includes 500 stocks. The Dow Jones Industrial Average is the narrowest measure of the market with only 30 stocks.

457. (D) Only answer D would improve the U.S. balance of payments. Foreign companies investing in the United States bring an inflow of funds, which improves the capital account of the balance of payments. Americans investing abroad, American companies building plants abroad, and banks lending to foreign companies all increase the outflow of funds and worsen (result in lowering U.S. reserves account) the U.S. balance of payments.

458. (A) Option III is the only incorrect statement. Treasury stock must have been authorized and issued by the corporation in order to have been traded on the market and available for the company to buy back. When a company buys back its own stock, it has no effect on the number of shares authorized. The other three statements are correct.

459. (B) The liquidity of a company is measured by the ease with which a company can turn over its current assets into cash to pay off its current liabilities. Both the quick ratio and net working capital give insight into the company's ability to turn over its current assets into cash to pay off its current liabilities. The quick ratio is current assets minus current liabilities, which is then divided by current liabilities. Net working capital is current assets minus current liabilities.

460. (A) The only transaction that decreases working capital is declaring a dividend because retained earnings is debited and dividends payable (a current liability) is credited. Paying a dividend has no effect on working capital because the debit and credit cancel each other out: cash is reduced by the same amount as the dividends payable account. The other two transactions do not affect current assets or current liabilities.

461. (D) Changes in inventories, money supply, and stock market prices are all leading indicators of the economy. Gross domestic product is not a leading indicator but a coincident indicator.

462. (D) The only defensive company stocks are utility companies. The stocks of the other three companies are cyclical.

463. (A) Primary earnings per share is $1.03 as calculated below:

Interest expense (6 percent bonds)	$300,000
(8 percent conv. bonds)	$800,000
	$1,100,000
Earnings before interest and taxes	$6,000,000
Minus interest expense	$1,100,000
Earnings before taxes	$4,900,000

$\downarrow$

Minus taxes (34 percent)	$1,666,000
Net income	$3,234,000

$\downarrow$

Minus preferred dividends	$150,000
Earnings available to common shareholders	$3,084,000

Number of common shares   3,000,000

$$\text{Earnings per share} = \frac{\text{earnings available to common shares}}{\text{number of common shares}}$$

$$= \frac{\$3,084,000}{3,000,000} = \$1.03$$

464. (C) Diluted earnings per share is $1.13 as calculated below:

Earnings before interest and taxes	$6,000,000
Minus interest expense (6 percent bonds)	$300,000
Earnings before taxes	$5,700,000

$\downarrow$

Minus taxes (34 percent)	$1,938,000
Net income	$3,762,000

$\downarrow$

Minus preferred dividends	$150,000
Earnings available to common shareholders	$3,612,000

Number of common shares   3,200,000

$$\text{Earnings per share} = \frac{\text{earnings available to common shares}}{\text{number of common shares}}$$

$$= \frac{\$3,612,000}{3,200,000} = \$1.13$$

465. (C) Value stocks are the stocks of companies that traditionally have low P/E ratios and are considered to be good value because there may be factors that cause them to be temporarily out of value. Many value companies pay dividends.

466. (D) Land cannot be depreciated. If, however, the land has minerals, mining rights, or agricultural value, the value of these assets may be depleted.

467. (A) The Federal Reserve Bank is least likely to purchase securities when wages are rising. Purchasing securities pumps money into the economy, which could exacerbate rising wage inflation. In such a situation the Fed is more likely to sell securities to reduce the money supply to combat rising wages, which could be the beginning of rising inflation. The Federal Reserve Bank would purchase securities to stimulate the economy when unemployment is increasing, interest rates are declining, or gross domestic product is declining.

468. (D) When a company issues convertible debt, the company's net working capital is increased when the proceeds from the issue are put into cash. Leverage is also increased from the issuance of a new convertible debt issue. When the bonds are issued, the proceeds are deposited into cash, which increases liquidity. There is an increased potential for the convertible bonds to be converted into common stock, which could dilute earnings per share.

469. (C) To calculate the coverage ratio, you need to obtain earnings before interest and taxes (EBIT) from the income statement. Then EBIT is divided by bond interest to calculate the debt coverage ratio.

470. (A) Convertible preferred stock, new issues of common stock, and warrants all have the potential for diluting earnings per share. Call options do not dilute earnings per share as they trade on outstanding shares.

471. (C) A head and shoulders top formation is bearish and best described as a reversal of a bullish trend.

472. (D) Direct participation programs or limited partnerships are the least liquid of the investments mentioned because it takes time to buy and sell them. In addition, investors need to be prequalified and also need to be accepted by the general partner before buying. Good quality stocks, Treasury bills, and mutual funds are liquid investments because they can be easily bought and sold. Stocks and Treasury bills are traded in active markets, and mutual funds are traded at the closing price at the end of the day at their net asset values for no-load funds and their offer prices for load funds.

473. (B) There is an inverse relationship between prices of existing bonds and interest rates. When interest rates rise, existing bond prices fall. When interest rates rise, more foreign money flows into the United States, making the U.S. dollar stronger. Strength in the U.S. dollar makes imports into the United States cheaper, hence, more competitive.

474. (C) When new stock is issued, equity increases and cash from the stock is increased. Cash is part of current assets, quick assets, and total assets, which all increase. Net worth is also increased because total liabilities are deducted from the increased current assets.

475. (C) Changing the discount rate (the rate charged by the Fed to banks for loans), changing reserve requirements (the percentage amounts that banks must keep on reserve) and participating in open-market operations (buying and selling U.S. securities in the bond markets) are all tools used by the Fed to control the money supply. The prime rate is not a tool of the Fed. It is the rate charged by banks to their best customers for loans.

476. (D) Of the choices only AAA-rated bonds and blue-chip stocks fit the description of good quality investments for a defensive strategy. Call options and high-yield bonds are riskier securities that are not suitable for a defensive investment strategy for a retiree.

477. (A) The support level is the lower portion of the trading range of the stock. The resistance level is the upper portion of the trading range of the stock.

478. (C) A technical analyst would view the market as overbought and would probably recommend that investors sell their stocks.

479. (D) Small investors trade in odd lots (less than 100 share trades), and the odd-lot theory professes small investors to be mostly wrong in their investment decisions. Thus, those that follow the odd-lot theory will sell when small investors are buying and buy when small investors are selling.

480. (A) Cash flow is determined by taking net income and adding back the noncash charges, such as depreciation and depletion. Cash flow = net income + depreciation + depletion.

481. (D) Countercyclical stocks move in the opposite direction to the economy. Cyclical stocks move in the same direction as the economy. Growth stocks are stocks of companies with high P/E ratios and high growth rates of sales, market share, or earnings. Blue-chip stocks are the stocks of established companies that are leaders in their fields with a history of good earnings and dividends.

482. (C) Defensive company stocks are those companies that maintain their value or do well in an economy that is declining. Companies such as tobacco, pharmaceutical, alcohol, and food tend to do well when the economy turns down.

483. (C) The market has a beta coefficient of 1, so a stock with a beta coefficient of less than 1 will be less volatile than the market. When the market goes up such a stock will go up less than the market. In this list, LMN stock with a beta coefficient of 1.75 should move up more than the market when stocks increase. A stock with a P/E ratio of 5 is a value stock and is not likely to increase as much as a growth stock.

484. (B) In order to get the earnings available to common shareholders to be able to calculate the earnings per share, you need to do the following:

Net sales	$15,000,000
Minus cost of goods sold	$5,000,000
Gross profit	$10,000,000

↓

Minus operating expenses	$4,000,000
Earnings before interest and taxes	$6,000,000

↓

Minus interest expenses	$500,000
Earnings before taxes	$5,500,000

↓

Minus taxes (50 percent)	$2,750,000
Earnings	$2,750,000

↓

Minus preferred dividends	$750,000
Earnings available to common shareholders	$2,000,000

$$\text{Earnings per share} = \frac{\text{earnings available to common shareholders}}{\text{number of common shares outstanding}}$$

$$= \frac{\$2,000,000}{1,000,000} = \$2.00$$

485. (A) *Systematic risk* is synonymous with *market risk.* When the stock market declines, prices of most stocks fall, and when the market rises, most stocks go up, even poor quality stocks.

486. (D) Quick assets include some current assets such as cash, marketable securities, and accounts receivable, which can be quickly converted into cash. Inventory is not a quick asset because it takes longer to sell and to be converted into cash.

487. (C) M2 money supply includes M1 (checking accounts, currency, and NOW accounts) plus time deposits, savings deposits, and money market accounts. Jumbo CDs are part of M3.

488. (A) The times interest ratio is determined by using the total interest expense (obtained from the income statement) divided into earnings before interest and taxes (EBIT or operating income) also obtained from the income statement. Information is obtained from the balance sheet for the other three ratios.

489. (B) The beta coefficient was developed to measure the volatility of a security in relation to the volatility of the market. The market always has a beta coefficient of 1, and so a stock with a beta of 1 would equal the volatility of the market. A beta coefficient of less than 1 indicates that the stock would be less volatile than the market. A stock with a beta greater than 1 would likely be more volatile than the market.

490. (C) A company with a high debt-to-assets ratio has financed a high portion of its assets with debt. A creditor would be concerned that if revenues drop, the company might not be able to service its debt and the risk of bankruptcy rises. The creditor would then have to stand in line to get paid. A high quick ratio indicates high liquidity, which a creditor wants to see. A low P/E ratio indicates that investors are paying a low multiple of earnings for the stock price. A high accounts receivable turnover indicates that those owing the company money are paying off their accounts quickly, which is what a creditor would want to see.

491. (D) A stock split indicates that the number of shares have been increased and affects the par value of the stock. There is no entry to record a stock split, and so the shareholder's equity, retained earnings, and additional paid-in capital remain unchanged.

492. (B) Last year the company's P/E ratio was 20 ($30/$1.50). If the P/E ratio remains the same for this year and the company earns $2 per share, then the price should be $40 per share ($2 × 20).

493. (A) Net worth remains unchanged because cash is increased by the same amount as the amount of the debt issued.

494. (A) The company pays out $0.50 per share (10% × $5), and the dividend yield is 2 percent ($0.50/$25)

495. (B) A company does not pay dividends to itself. Therefore, the 100,000 treasury shares that the company owns are deducted from the outstanding shares (800,000 − 100,000 = 700,000 shares) and then divided into the amount of money to be distributed to shareholders ($320,000/700,000), which equals dividends of $0.46 per share.

496. (A) When there is a decline in short positions, there are fewer open positions in the stock, which gives less support to the particular stock. Therefore, a technical analyst would view this information as bearish on the stock.

497. (C) The consumer price index (CPI) is the best indicator to measure inflation or deflation. Gross domestic product (GDP) is the total of all goods and services produced in a country in one year. A narrow measure of the money supply, M1 includes coins and currency in circulation, checking accounts, and NOW accounts. The currency exchange rate is the rate at which one currency is converted into another currency.

498. (D) The only money market security in the list that trades with accrued interest is CDs. Treasury bills, commercial paper, and bankers' acceptances are issued at a discount and mature at par value. An investor purchasing a CD would have to pay the seller any accrued interest due.

499. (C) The only ratio that cannot be determined from the balance sheet is earnings per share, which requires income available to common shareholders. Earnings are found in the income statement.

500. (A) A fundamental analyst is not concerned with market timing because the work of a fundamental analyst is to determine what stocks to buy and not when to buy them. All of the other answers are used by a fundamental analyst.